RIGHT-WING
COLLECTIVISM

THE OTHER THREAT TO LIBERTY

Preface by Deirdre McCloskey | **JEFFREY TUCKER**

FEE FOUNDATION *for*
ECONOMIC EDUCATION

FEE's mission is to inspire, educate, and connect future leaders with the economic, ethical, and legal principles of a free society.

Find us online at:

FEE.org

Facebook.com/FEEonline

Twitter.com/FEEonline (@feeonline)

Foundation for Economic Education
1819 Peachtree Road NE, Suite 300
Atlanta, Georgia 30309

Telephone: (404) 554-9980

ISBN (ebook): 978-1-63069-608-5

ISBN (print): 978-1-57246-299-1

2017

Published under the Creative Commons Attribution 4.0 International License by The Foundation for Economic Education

*Jann & Matt
Christmas 2019*

Right-Wing Collectivism

The Other Threat to Liberty

Jeffrey Tucker

— FEE.org —

Contents

IV. The Philosophy

V. The Future

To the socialists of all parties

Preface

We call it "populism." That makes it sounds even a little good, at any rate to people who cannot remember the past. Why shouldn't the will of the *people* trump all? Surely the result of a vote is the *volonté generale*, said Rousseau, believing he had thereby solved the problem of un-freedom in a collective. Surely populism is a Good and General Thing? So one might feel, at any rate until vague memories of Huey Long and Juan Peron and Benito Mussolini crowd in.

Jeffrey Tucker in his brilliant book calls right-wing populism what it actually is, namely, fascism, or, in its German form national socialism, nazism. "Fascism" has of course been corrupted by its promiscuous use on the left, as by Anti-Fas nihilists in Berkeley throwing rocks and insults at the police and the non-violent protestors against President Trump's latest. Tucker dusts off the word for present use. It's exactly the word we need. Urgently.

In elegant prose and deep history Tucker tells the story of how the twin anti-liberal, fathered c. 1820 by Georg Hegel, parted company. Prussia and Russia, you might say. Anything but England. The twin on the right, from Carlyle and recently Breitbart News, elevated the state with nationalism. The twin on the left, from Marx and recently MSNBC, elevated the state with socialism. Either way, the state, with its monopoly of violence, was elevated. English liberalism—which meanwhile gave us our liberties and then our riches—elevated instead the individual people and their voluntary agreements. As the ur-liberal Adam Smith put it in 1776, what we need, and for a while what we got, imperfectly, was "the liberal plan, of equality [in social standing], liberty [in economic action], and justice [in legal standing]."

Tucker raises the alarm against Trumpian Putinism worldwide, from Hungary to the Philippines. He denies the myth that "fascism" is out of date because it was bravely defeated in 1945 by the left. Our friends on the left (I speak sincerely: I have many) imagine they are still fighting a fascism in alliance with friendly Uncle Joe Stalin puffing on his pipe. Actually they are practicing a left version of fascism. As George Orwell discovered in the Spanish Civil War, and recorded in *Animal Farm*, the left is fully as authoritarian as the right. Both use the state's power to push people around. As Tucker documents, after 1989 the greatest threat of pushing around is as much from the right as from the left. The fascist threat comes not from a Berliner but from a Trumpian Wall.

A true liberalism breaks down walls, of tyranny and tariffs as much as migration and censorship and occupational licensure. It stands against both of the authoritarian twins and their splendid walls. Tucker urges the humane liberals to stand up, and get straight their people-centered principles. He urges them to stop believing that they are "conservative" and should therefore tolerate a little the drift into fascism, the better to get tax reform.

A host at MSNBC harassed a fellow from the libertarian Cato Institute, whom he tagged as "conservative," and did not let him speak. The guest squeezed in a brief protest that he was *not* a conservative. The point got lost, and the show broke for a commercial. The man from Cato, and Jeffrey Tucker (the man from the Foundation for Economic Education), and Rose Wilder Lane and Friedrich Hayek and Milton Friedman are all liberals, not conservatives, not progressives. The liberals stand against the twins of violently enforced state action.

Still, the ugly, violent twins remain popular. The fresh popularity of the fascist twin worries Tucker. It should worry you.

Why on both left and right, one might ask, is the state the central actor in the political and economic drama. Why is it the drama most people love?

One reason, first, is ancient, the primitive suspicion we have that a deal in the market is unfair. The suspicion made some sense in the zero-sum world in which most people lived until the nineteenth century. The sociologist Georg Simmel put it well in 1907: "The masses— from the Middle Ages right up to the nineteenth century—thought that there was something wrong with the origin of great fortunes.... Tales of horror spread about the origin of the Grinaldi, the Medici, and the Rothschild fortunes ... as if a demonic spirit was at work." It is the masses, the populists, *hoi polloi*, who hold such views vividly. A jailer in the thirteenth century scorned a rich man's pleas for mercy: "Come, Master Arnaud Teisseire, you have wallowed in such opulence! ... How could you be without sin?"

Yet in a voluntary deal you the demander and he the supplier both gain. Both profit. Win-win. In the nature of mutual gain, however, each could possibly have got *more* gain. There's always that annoying gap. The man in the street calls the gain achieved by his suppliers of groceries and housing their "profit," and resents that he can't shift more of it to himself. He does not reflect that he himself is earning a species of profit—or else he would not have agreed to the sale in the first place. From a supplier's point of view, the demander is himself a profiteer. Both sides are. Marshallian economists call the gap between willingness to pay and willingness to accept "the sum of consumer's and producer's surplus." Marxists call it, more vividly, and with disapproval, "exploitation" or "surplus value." Anyway it is the social gain from trade—the value created by trade—to be divided somehow into your profit from the transaction and the supplier's. We grumble. Did I get the best deal I could? Has he made a fool of me? He is a vicious profiteer. Why doesn't he gracefully give me more?

When democracy began to flourish and hierarchy began to die we start believing that there's a solution handily available. The ancient prejudice against trade generates a modern notion that the state will fix it, giving us all the dignity and sustenance we require. (No one in 1600 believed such an absurdity, because it was obvious that the state was a band of robbers into whose clutches we had fallen.) From a single citizen's point of view, indeed, the state's gifts *do* seem like wonderful free lunches. Roads. Public schools. A nice post office, with a friendly postman. They just appear. No cost. No wretched bargaining, or work.

And, second, such a fantasy of a benevolent state handing out costless goodies, whether run by an imagined central planner in socialism or by an imagined *Führer* in nationalism, has another (and now exclusively modern) narrative support. The new narrative leans against the economic truth that the modern world comes out of fantastically ramified trade with strangers. "No, no," replies the new narrative. "We are all members of a loving family at home. Let's go forward together."

When we all lived on farms, and knew where meat came from, no one dreamed of socialism. We knew that market prices mattered, and could make or break our lives. We knew that income came from work. We knew on our pulses the truth of diminishing returns and the universality of scarcity. My students from farms or small businesses in which the children participated are able to understand economics swiftly. The others, including myself, are not. When incomes began to come massively if mysteriously from The Office we began to think that the problem was not production but distribution, as at a loving family's dinner table. Pass the potatoes, Helen. Certainly, John. Have some more.

Swedish politics in 1928 was transformed from liberalism to a tentative socialism when Per Albin Hansson gave his classic speech in Parliament recommending *folkhemmet*, "the people's home": "There is equality, consideration, cooperation and helpfulness in the good home. Applied to the greater home of people and citizens, this would mean breaking down all the social and economic barriers that now separate citizens into privileged and neglected [categories], ruling and dependent, rich and poor, propertied and impoverished, plunderers and exploited."

When a generous modern child first realizes how very poor the people are in the next neighborhood, she naturally wishes to open her wallet, or still better Daddy's wallet. It is at such an age—fourteen or sixteen—that we form political identities, which we seldom then revise in the face of later evidence. By contrast, in an ancient hierarchical society of slaves and owners the slave-owning child had no such guilt, because the poor were fated to be slavish. But once the naturalness of hierarchy was questioned, as it was during the eighteenth century in northwestern Europe, it was a short step to socialism or, if you prefer, after a while, national socialism. Our families are little socialist economies, with Mom as central planner. Neat.

"Amoral familism," observed the political scientist Edward Banfield in 1958, characterizes a pre-modern society. It protects family members, but cheats and murders everyone else. Consult the long-form TV show of 1999–2007, *The Sopranos*. A modern society in its authoritarian version expands the family to the nation, the *folkhem*. We cheat the bosses and murder the enemies, *en masse*.

You need Tucker's book. You need to worry. If you are a real liberal, you need to know where the new national socialism comes from, the better to call it out and shame it back into the shadows. Now.

— Deirdre Nansen McCloskey

Introduction

On August 11–12, 2017, in Charlottesville, Virginia, hundreds of mostly young men gathered in the center of the town once frequented by Thomas Jefferson. They were carrying torches, waving Nazi and white supremacist flags, and issuing genocidal threats to whole groups. They were there ostensibly to protest the removal of a statue of General Robert E. Lee, as voted on by the city council.

But according to organizers, the purpose of the "Unite the Right" rally was broader. It was to be an unveiling of a new movement. The use of the term "right" here is fascinating because the organizers considered this term inclusive of the Ku Klux Klan and self-described Nazis. The presentation they made was something of a trauma for many people—even all over the world—because few had fully understood the violent and destructive social forces that had been simmering beneath the surface of American life until that day.

What is this thing we have encountered, this strange movement that is alive and growing in Europe and the United States? What do these people want? What is their ideological origin? Can it really be considered "right wing," and, if so, in what respect? This book seeks to answer these questions.

The rise of the so-called alt-right is the most unexpected ideological development of our time. Most people of the current generation lack a sense of the historical sweep of the intellectual side of the right-wing collectivist position. It represents the revival of a tradition of interwar collectivist thought that might at first seem like a hybrid but was distinctly mainstream between the two world wars. It is anti-communist but not for the reasons that were conventional during the Cold War, that is, because communism opposed freedom in the liberal tradition. Right-collectivism also opposes traditional liberalism. It opposes free trade, freedom of association, free migration, and capitalism understood as a laissez-faire free market. It rallies around nation and state as the organizing principles of the social order—and trends in the direction of favoring one-man rule—but positions itself as opposed to leftism traditionally understood.

We know about certain fascist leaders from the mid-20th century, but not the ideological orientation that led to them or the ideas they left on the table to be picked up generations later. For the most part, and until recently, it seemed to have dropped from history. Meanwhile, the prospects for social democratic ideology are fading, and something else is coming to fill that vacuum. What is it? Where does it come from? Where is it leading?

This book seeks to fill the knowledge gap, to explain what this movement is about and why anyone who genuinely loves and longs for liberty classically understood needs to develop a nose and instinct for spotting the opposite when it comes in an unfamiliar form. We need to learn to recognize the language, the thinkers, the themes, the goals of a political ethos that is properly identified as fascist.

Why the designation "right wing"? It's a fair question, because the history of right and left is enormously complicated and the definitions are always changing. If by left, you mean anything trending toward despotism, and, if by right, you mean anything trending toward freedom, my use of the term "right wing" here will make no sense to you. But that leaves us with a problem. It doesn't make much sense to describe, for example, both Karl Marx and Carl Schmitt as "left wing" when Schmitt's entire ideological apparatus was constructed in overt opposition to Marx. And it doesn't account for why some of the most successful tyrannies of the 20th century rose in opposition to communism and turned out to be just as dangerous as the thing they opposed.

I will argue for the designation of "right wing" on grounds that these movements appropriate certain rightist themes for despotic ends. They denounce the decadent and "degenerate" left and speak about family, faith, nation, and even property. But this rhetoric is not deployed in the interest of bourgeois freedom but rather as political rhetoric designed to rally a specific middle-class demographic to their side. They can rail against the leftist takeover of media and academy with the best of them, but their interest is not in allowing maximum personal and economic liberty but rather constraining both in the service of nation, state, blood, soil, throne, and altar. Most often these people are granted motive force by the perception that leftism is on the rise and needs to be combated; indeed, that is the origin of the fascist movements of the last 100 years. But what they want instead is something other than freedom; it is a new form of comprehensive social and economic control.

A distinct trait of right-wing collectivism is its obsession with demographics. This fits with the overall ideology, which is focused not on class but deep identity issues that frequently default to race and ethnicity. Ludwig von Mises wrote of Nazism in 1947 that "It aimed at abolishing laissez-faire not only in the production of material goods, but no less in the production of men." This is true of most forms of fascism: it goes after hard targets, through a variety of means from migration controls to eugenics to birth planning and procreation control. Anarchy in the production of people is not tolerated. In a strange way, this makes sense. If you seek to control the social order, really control it, you have to start with controlling population demographics.

Our generation has little real-world experience to deal with reactionary movements and their effects. What I will try to show is that such rightist thought has deep roots tracing to the early 19th century, when the followers of Hegel split into right and left branches, depending on whether one believed that the Prussian state and church did or did not provide the end point of cultural evolution. The rightists went one way and the left went another. They both pushed a revolt against the liberal upheaval that fundamentally changed the social and demographic structure of Western society. Right and left, in many different national experiences, proposed different ways to deal with what they regarded as a disaster in the making. Each had its own version of revanchism, that is, an agenda focused on reclaiming previously conquered territory they believe was taken away, a demand to put back under control what has been lost to freedom. To put it another way, these are the people who wanted to dig up the body of Adam Smith and hang him in effigy.

What I'm calling right-wing collectivism really does represent a semi-coherent tradition of thought: the language, themes, resentments, answers, and visions are consistent for some two hundred years, intensifying by the decade. I trace this tradition in the course of this book.

I do want to add a caveat on the matter of Donald Trump, mostly because some chapters herein address his outlook and administration. I have been outspoken in explaining the quasi-fascist origins of some features of his policies. The book republishes an essay I wrote July 2015, just as the campaign for president opened. I had just finished re-reading Mises's *Omnipotent Government* from 1944, his most focused and extended discussion of fascist/Nazi ideology. The parallels in thematics and policy were remarkably similar. It was this day that I realized that much more needed to be said on this. However, it would be too easy to characterize this book as an oppositional tract. It is not. Not everything he favors is bad and not everything that the administration pushes should be opposed. Indeed, to the extent that any leader or regime favors any degree of deregulation or tax cuts (ideas tossed out much later in the campaign), or more peaceful foreign relations, that is something that any adherent of traditional liberalism should favor, regardless of partisan issues. But what is at the core of the governing philosophy and what is a superficial add on to make the rest palpable to as many people as possible? This is the more profound question.

What I'm urging is a greater awareness of the ideology we are dealing with here, and a greater consciousness on the part of supporters of freedom that they are not actually part of the left/right spectrum, with a particular focus on the most neglected part of that spectrum. Once you understand this, books like F.A. Hayek's *Road to Serfdom* (1944) make much more sense. His warning concerned the symbiotic relationship between left and right forms of totalitarianism, and the failure dynamic between them.

In 1956 (the date is significant), FEE's founder Leonard Read wrote the following:

> "Left" and "right" are each descriptive of authoritarian positions. Liberty has no horizontal relationship to authoritarianism. Libertarianism's relationship to authoritarianism is vertical; it is up from the muck of men enslaving man.... What, actually, is the difference between communism and fascism? Both are forms of statism, authoritarianism. The only difference between Stalin's communism and Mussolini's fascism is an insignificant detail in organizational structure. But one is "left" and the other is "right"! Where does this leave the libertarian in a world of Moscow word-making? The libertarian is, in reality, the opposite of the communist. Yet, if the libertarian employs the terms "left" and "right," he is falling into the semantic trap of being a "rightist" (fascist) by virtue of not being a "leftist" (communist). This is a semantic graveyard for libertarians, a word device that excludes their existence. While those with Moscow relations will continue this theme, there is every reason why libertarians should avoid it.

What Read most likely could not have imagined is that this terminology would survive the Cold War and come roaring back in the 21st century. What's more, he would be shocked to see so many libertarians of our time thoroughly confused about where we fit within the left/right structure. The answer is that we do not. But to see that requires that we know more.

And keep in mind, this is not just an intellectual parlor game. We are at a turning point in the history of freedom. We have the technology today to enable unprecedented freedom and empowerment for all. We have legacy states that are holding us back. We have power structures looking for a rationale for their rule. As I argue in this book, the social democratic welfare/planning state is tired, spent, and increasingly unpopular. The question is: what will replace it? Will it be freedom or some differently branded form of social and economic control? This is why right-wing collectivism matters right now. It is vying for the position of becoming a ruling ideological structure that can delay and reverse the progress we are making (mostly through technology rather than political change) toward universal freedom. It seems inconceivable that we could repeat the history of the interwar years in a slightly different form but nothing is impossible when bad ideas win out over good ones.

* * * *

During the last two years, the pages of FEE.org (of which I'm the editor) have covered this topic in detail. Most of the essays in this book first appeared in some form at FEE as part of its daily content. I can speak for all the contributors of FEE in offering a special note of thanks to the board, donors, staff, and readers of FEE for the support for this great institution, which has maintained its principled stand for liberty since its founding in 1946.

In addition, many people have contributed mightily to my own understanding of this topic, through ongoing suggestions for reading. There are too many to name but I would like to make special mention of intellectual assistance from Danny Sanchez, Lawrence Reed, Wayne Olson, Richard Lorenc, Tom Palmer, Stephan Kinsella, Laurie Rice, Steve Horwitz, Jonah Goldberg, Thomas Leonard, Deirdre McCloskey, and countless numbers of commentators on social media who have provided continual feedback.

We are living in hard times for liberal philosophy. We can overcome them only through greater understanding of our past struggles and future challenges. True lovers of human ennoblement through freedom need a greater consciousness of who we are, what we've achieved in the past, and what it is going to take to make a rational and persuasive case against both left and right, and for something beautiful and true that can renew the face of the earth.

— Jeffrey A. Tucker

I
THE SCENE

The Violence in Charlottesville

The vast majority of people in the United States have no interest whatsoever in street battles between the alt-right (better described today in more poignant terms) and the counter-protesters. Most people have normal problems like paying bills, dealing with kids, getting health care, keeping life together under all the usual strains, and mostly want these weird people to go away. So, of course, people are shocked at scenes of young people in the streets of this picturesque town with a university founded by Thomas Jefferson screaming, "Jews will not replace us."

It's hard to see, hard to hear. But they are not going away. For some people with heads full of violent ideology, what's happened so far is not enough. They imagine that with their marches, flags, uniforms, slogans, chants, screams, and guns, they will cause history to erupt and dramatically turn to favor them over the people they hate. Indeed, what is unfolding right now, with real loss of property and life, has gone beyond politics as usual and presages something truly terrible from the past, something most of us had previously believed was unrepeatable.

What in the world causes such a thing? It's not about bad people as such. Many of the young men and women involved in this movement were raised in good homes and, under normal conditions, would never hurt anyone. What this is about is bad ideas. They crawl into the brain and cause people to imagine things that do not exist. It can be like a disease that a person doesn't even know that he or she has. It causes people to seethe with hatred for no apparent reason, to long for the extermination of people who have never done anything wrong, to imagine insane outcomes of social struggles that have zero chance of succeeding.

The Group

The implausibility of their ideas is disguised by group psychology. They hang around people who think these same things and egg each other on in shared resentments and dreams of new powers they can acquire if they act boldly, bravely, and with determination. They conjure up scapegoats (blacks, Jews, women, Antifa, gays, and a government that is supposedly giving them all privileges at their expense) and begin to believe that the only way forward is to destroy them all in some grand uprising, after which they will seize power and rule forever.

Yes, I know it sounds insane. But one thing you learn from history is that no idea is too insane to be off limits to a group infected with a longing to rule. Any means to the end will do, with the end deeply embedded in the fevered imagination of the group member who finds mission, meaning, and significance from some struggle.

The Statue Myth

Much of the media coverage about the violence in Charlottesville, Virginia report that this all began with a dispute over the fate of a statue of the Civil War Confederate general Robert E. Lee that sits downtown. The city council voted to take it down; the protesters want it to remain as a symbol of white pride and rule (which is absurd because General Lee would have been thoroughly repulsed by the ideology these people represent). In actual fact, the dispute over this statue is a complete distraction from the real motivation here.

What this really is: an explosive expression of an idea that has been brewing in a malevolent movement that has been gaining steam for very a long time. After the Second World War, most people imagined that Nazi ideology was gone from the earth and that the only real totalitarian view that remained to threaten liberty was Communism. That might have been true for a few decades, but matters began to change in the 1990s, as new violent strains of statism begin to arise.

The Deep History

For the last two years, I've written about the deep history of this violent strain, which can be described variously as Nazism, fascism, alt-right, white supremacy, white nationalism, neo-reaction, or, my preferred and more technical moniker (borrowed from Ludwig von Mises), right-Hegelianism.

People have variously wondered why I've spent so much time and energy digging through the works of people like Johann Fichte, Friedrich List, Houston Stewart Chamberlain, Thomas Carlyle, John Ruskin, Charles Davenport, Oswald Spengler, Carl Schmitt, Julius Evola, Giovanni Gentile, and so on. All of these ideas existed long before Hitler and the Nazis—and caused enormous damage in the world long before the Holocaust—and they persist after them.

It's true that probably not even one of the protesters in Charlottesville have read these thinkers, much less the traditional liberal response to these rightist strain of anti-liberalism. How can they possibly be responsible?

Ideas are strangely magical, like time-traveling spiritual DNA, moving from brain to brain like a genetic mutation and just as unpredictably. Keynes was right to observe that most politicians are slaves to some defunct economist; in the same way these violent thugs are slaves to some defunct philosopher who loathed the emergence of universal freedom in the world during the 19th century and were determined to set it back.

Propagandists for Evil

At the same time, there must be some mode of transmission for ideas. The leaders of this movement serve the purpose well, but there is a deeper root. I've been very reluctant to mention what might be the most influential tract among the rise of the hard statist right in the last few decades, but given where we are with all of this, it is time. The book is *The Turner Diaries*, written by "Andrew McDonald" who was really William L. Pierce, a brilliant physicist whose mind was taken over by Nazi ideology, precisely because he was steeped in the literature above.

I do not recommend reading this book. You can't unread it. It is their roadmap. I can recall the first time I read it. I was shaken to my very core, and it was the beginning of a new realization of the task before us, to combat this horror with every bit of intellectual energy.

It is the story of a small junta of whites who set out to reverse history with a series of killings, starting with Jews, then blacks, then communists, and then, inevitably, apologists for the merchant class and libertarians (they hate us deeply too). What you learn early on here is that this movement is absolutely socialist, just in a different way from the more-famous left-wing socialists. They are not red shirts but brown shirts, so they have a different agenda. It's not about class struggle. It's about race struggle, religious struggle, gender identity struggle, national struggle.

So what happens? They rally the masses to their side with a growing amount of bloodshed, gain control of the government, set up a centrally planned socialist state, get hold of the nuclear stockpile and slaughter all non-whites in the world. Sorry for the spoiler.

The Genetic Code

Why would anyone rally behind such a ghastly book? Again, the human mind is capable of imagining terrible things, and that which we imagine to be true influences actions. Ideas, as they say, have consequences. Hence, anyone who has followed the transmission of these ideas over the last decades could see where this is heading.

What happens now? The tragedy is compounded, with a burgeoning leftist movement to counter the emerging threat from the opposite side, and a government ready to exploit the conflict between the two to crack down further on human rights and freedoms. It's the perfect storm.

Our Task

The question is: what to do now? The answer lies in the source of the problem. The huge mess began with bad ideas. The only means available—and it is the most powerful—is to fight bad ideas with good ideas. We all need to throw ourselves into the intellectual battle most of all and as never before. What are those good ideas?

The progress of the last 500 years shows us precisely what the good ideas are: social harmony, human rights, the aspiration of universal dignity, the conviction that we can work together in mutual advantage, the market economy as a means of peace and prosperity, and, above all else, the beauty and magnificence of the idea of liberty itself.

Let us all—those who love peace, prosperity, and human flourishing for all—not despair but rather rededicate ourselves to the mission of replacing bad ideas with good ones. Our predecessors in this mission faced far worse odds and they prevailed, and they were far fewer than us. We can too, provided we think, speak, and act with courage and conviction in favor of all that is beautiful and true. This is how the left/right cycle of violence will be replaced by the highest longings of the human heart.

Lessons from the Charlottesville March

I t's a rule of social and political movements that they cannot fully control the outcome of their efforts. Actions cause reactions, many of them unanticipated and certainly unintended. This is because no group, no matter how powerful, can control the human minds of others not part of their cause.

This is why so many movements driven by a revolt ethos and revolutionary intentions have created so many unforeseen messes that are often the opposite of their stated aims.

So it is with the "Unite the Right" (alt-right, fascist, white supremacist, revanchist, Nazi, and so on) marchers who descended on the peaceful Virginia town of Charlottesville in August.

Donald Trump and many others like to say that there were "good people" marching too, but this ignores the entire title of the rally. The "Unite the Right" theme meant that anyone participating was necessarily putting aside differences with the Nazis and the Klan in order to achieve the goal of becoming a national political presence (the controversy over the statue of Robert E. Lee was only the excuse).

The aftermath of the march has been a fallout very different from what they expected.

Statues Torn Down

Only a few years ago, the idea of toppling the statues of Confederate generals strewn throughout the South would have been unthinkable. Charlottesville was a test case: perhaps this Lee statue should go, simply because it seems to be a distraction from the progress the citizens want and an unnecessary reminder of a painful past. The city council voted to remove it. This precipitated the rally.

To be sure, there are defensible arguments for recognizing the Confederate dead. But the protesters were not drawn from a heritage society like the Sons of Confederate Veterans (my great-grandfather was a medic in a Southern troop, and I'm named after Jefferson Davis), but rather the hardest and most bitter among the hard-right, anti-liberal ideologues. That association has further fueled the anti-statue movement among activists, and today none are safe. They are being torn down in the dead of night, all over the country, stricken down by city councils all over the South, and condemned as never before. None will likely survive this.

Should the statues stay or not? These statues have a complex history. They were not erected to honor the Confederate dead following the war or even at the end of Reconstruction. Most appeared in the early 1920s to send a message that the race-relation liberalization that happened between 1880 and 1900 would not return. The progress and normalcy would be replaced by a racist/statist/"progressive" movement rallying around new eugenic laws, zoning, white supremacy, forced exclusion, state segregation and so on—policies supported not by the people but by white elites infected with demographic fear and pseudo-science. This is when a movement started putting up these statues, not to honor history but as a symbol of intimidation and state control of association.

The statue in Charlottesville statue went up the same year that immigration restrictions went into place for explicit eugenic reasons, and Jim Crow laws were tight and an entire population group faced what amounted to an attempted extermination (that is not an exaggeration but a description of a well-documented reality).

In other words, Lee (a tragic figure in many ways) was then being drafted by a wicked movement he would likely have never supported, despite all his failings. So the controversy over whether it should stay or go is not really about the war that occurred a half-century before the statue went up but a symbol of racial control. This is the memory we are dealing with here. It's very similar to how the Neo-Nazis today are abusing his tragic legacy in service of their dangerous agenda.

Public Revulsion

During the presidential campaign in 2015, Hillary Clinton famously attacked the "deplorables" who were supporting Trump, including hard racists and fascists. The result was outrage: it seemed that she was calling all Trump supporters these names. In fact, Trump supporters—so many were just people disgusted by the policies of his predecessor and wanted fundamental change in government—took on the name "deplorable."

Most people in those days—never forget that most regular people do not follow 4chan or Twitter—had no idea of the burgeoning movement of hard-right ideologues that was gathering at the time, using Trump for their own purposes.

The Charlottesville "Unite the Right" march changed everything. What we saw from online videos and news reports was what looked like a dangerous paramilitary force, none from the city, with optics from the interwar period, carrying torches, Nazi-style insignias, flags, and screaming anti-Semitic and racist slogans. This was not anything like a Tea Party protest. It was something completely different and truly terrifying for the residents of this idyllic town.

In other words, it looked deplorable. It was the breakout of this movement into the mainstream. But instead of fueling some kind of white revolution, the results have been the exact opposite. This movement seems anti-American, filled with hate, unchecked by normal civil engagement, truly dangerous to public order, and of strange foreign origin. This did not look like free speech; it looked like a threat. It was not about demanding freedom but rather demanding power.

This is what accounts for the shock and disorientation among conservative and Republican commentators who want nothing to do with these people and the ideas behind it. From my point of view, this is very good. From the point of view of this movement, it is presumably not what they were going for.

What's fascinating to me is how these people got to this point of no return, forgetting to check themselves with observations such as: "do you think it is wise that we parade around like the very people the US went to war to defeat only 70 years ago?"

To understand that requires we plunge into the kind of group psychology that leads to such fanatic movements—too much to take on here.

Government Crackdown

The marchers used Virginia's open-carry laws and protections for free speech and association to their advantage. They also used the plea for tolerating their ideas in order to get a hearing. The ACLU, I believe, was right in fighting for the speech rights of the marchers.

That said, this was not a march about human rights; it was a march about threats to others and a demand for power. It has prompted Justice Department investigations, a resignation from the board of the ACLU, and a widespread questioning of how this fiasco that resulted in so much mayhem was ever tolerated to begin with.

We are nearly guaranteed to see an increase in government surveillance of hate groups, of monitoring of our online communications, of restrictions on political organizing—all in reaction and response and to the cheers of a terrified public.

It is precisely events like this that cause people to lose freedoms, not gain them. If any participants in the "Unite the Right" really believed they were fighting for freedom, they have achieved the opposite. But there is also this: groups like this thrive in persecution. They never go away, especially this one because so much of its ethos is about how they have been suppressed and oppressed. Make them victims and they thrive ever more.

Boost to the Left

The true tragedy of many responses to the march was the false choice it set up: that the only alternative to the alt-right is the leftist antifa. Or conversely, if you hate the leftist antifa, you have no choice but to back the alt-right. This is sheer nonsense. Most of the people resisting what had all the appearances of a Nazi invasion were regular citizens, not antifa. There is nothing "leftist" about resenting the vision of Nazis taking over public spaces.

It was a true inspiration to see the response from the merchant class, condemning racism and fascism in no uncertain terms. Business loves peace and friendship, not hate and civil unrest.

However, politically, it is unclear whether this response will find a voice. The people most in opposition to the rise of the Nazi movement in America has been the left, and the fallout could actually boost the prospects of the Bernie Sanders movement, as revulsion leads to an embrace of its seeming opposite.

Incidentally, this is precisely why it is so important for libertarians to speak out with truth and courageous conviction. We simply cannot allow the left to be the only ideological voice of opposition.

Trump's Legacy

It is probably too early to say what will define Trump's legacy in office, but his defense of the marchers, and the equation of their bad elements with the other bad elements that opposed them, might be it. It was the very statement that the most indefensible aspects of the alt-right truly wanted. And it was thus no surprise that even some of Trump's previous defenders bailed on him in the days following.

You cannot give up your credibility on basic issues like human rights and the dignity of every human life and expect to maintain political support over the long run. We are too far down the path toward peace and universal emancipation to go there. The future is bright and not grim and bloody, as these marchers and their backers imagine.

Many people have predicted the end of the Trump approach before, but something does seem different this time. It's very sad because Trump has many good ideas—ideas that are evidently not that important to him—and represents too many good causes (for which he has done very little) for this to happen. But when you choose to die on a hill of bigotry and intolerance, there is not enough credibility remaining for anything else.

No movement based on the aspiration to rule and oppress others can fully anticipate how their activities will play out over time. In this respect, the alt-right has done a terrible disservice to itself and perhaps to everyone else as well.

The question is: what are people who love human rights and liberty for all going to do about it? In the end, the only really effective resistance comes in what we believe and how we live our lives. We have seen what we do not love. The real issue is whether we can find and then build what it is we truly do love.

My Lunch with a Nazi

College made me profoundly aware and disdainful of leftist socialist ideology. It was everywhere in every discipline: history, psychology, sociology, ethics, and even economics. The alternative I knew about was called "right wing" or conservatism/libertarianism.

These were the days of the Cold War. Everything was clear. To be pro-American meant to be pro-freedom and certainly not a leftist. The bad guys blamed America for everything and never stopped putting down freedom.

Where do the Nazis fit in here? They didn't matter in the slightest, except as a matter of history. I took a class in World War II. The impression I had was that Nazis were a cult that came out of nowhere, killed a lot of people, and were then vanquished by the Allied troops. And that was the end. There was little discussion of the ideological structure, its meaning, its import. It was just some weird junta that came and went.

Nazis Exist

That's where things stood until a very strange lunch in Alexandria, Virginia. Years had gone by. I was perhaps 26 years old. A journalist in Washington, D.C., an acquaintance with some odd views that I couldn't quite place, had arranged a meeting. He told me of a wealthy philanthropist who I really needed to meet. She could make some good connections for me.

I wasn't sure I understood what all this was about but I was up for it.

I arrived at the brightly lit and elegant tea room where the wait-staff were bustling around, serving high-end clientele. I sat and waited, and then a hand touched my shoulder.

"Jeffrey Tucker?"

"I am he," I said and stood up to greet a beautiful woman in her 60s, gorgeously dressed, blonde hair pinned up top. She had flawless manners, a pretty way of speaking, and all the signs of "high birth," as they say, on top of the classic "beauty that money buys." I held her chair and seated her. We ordered some small sandwiches and tea and began to talk.

We began with the problem of leftism and how terrible it all is. I was intrigued at the polished cadence of her language. And the way she moved her hands. And her bright and pretty eyes. Her perfume. And the way she smiled and connected with me so personally. I was enjoying this, feeling special.

The nature of the conversation began to shift gradually. The problem was not the left as such, she said, but the global elites. It is they who are behind the corruption of the culture through Hollywood and the media generally. Their power is bad enough, she explained, but the real problem is within the banking system and the world financial system that they own.

I didn't really understand what she meant by "they" but I didn't like every movie, so I was okay with a solid attack on Hollywood. And I certainly didn't like the Fed. I would respond in each case with a point about the problems of government. Each time, she would gently explain to me that the problem is not the government but the people who occupy the government who are building a world order to benefit only one tribe.

I still didn't entirely understand. Finally, she put a fine point on it.

"The real problem, Jeffrey, and I hope you can come to understand this more fully, is the Jews."

Ok, now I'm rolling my eyes. Here we go with the cranky stuff.

I've heard this kind of talk before but mostly from uncouth and uneducated malcontents who seem consumed by class resentment. It was boring and dumb. I must say, however, that I had never heard someone of her beauty and intelligence speak this way. I found it embarrassing more than anything.

I didn't argue with her, mostly because I wouldn't even have known where to begin. Mostly I had no real understanding of her outlook, where it came from, what it meant, where she was going with talk of this. In the world I grew up in, I had no consciousness of Jews or non-Jews or anything at all related to this topic.

Above all, I would stop and wonder: why am I having lunch with this person?

She shifted again to talk about her personal biography. Her husband left her a substantial amount of money. She set up her own philanthropic empire. She supported journalists, magazines, institutions, conferences. She is highly careful in her spending, she explained, making sure that she backs people and institutions who know both the problem and the answer.

Now I understood where this was going. She was recruiting me, testing me. Maybe if I studied and learned, and deepened the sophistication of my personal philosophy, I too could benefit from her generosity.

From there, things ramped up quickly. She said, "Well, that's enough serious talk. Let's offer a small toast to the greatest man of our century."

Maybe she meant Reagan? We lifted our glasses. Then she finally came out with it.

"Adolf Hilter."

Well, now that seemed to come from nowhere. I made a sheepish face and slowly lowered my glass. She knew that she had shocked me but gave a playful smile and engaged in more small talk. I wasn't listening anymore, simply because I was just a bit distracted by her toast.

At some point in the remaining minutes of this meeting I realized: I was having lunch with a real Nazi. It was not a frothing-at-the-mouth thug with a club and torch. It was a beautiful, erudite, and highly educated woman of high breeding.

Goodbyes

Fortunately, lunch time ended. We did air kisses and polite goodbyes and said we would stay in touch. I walked to my car as quickly as I could without seeming to rush. I sat down and exhaled as much air as I could and took another deep breath. What had just happened? Who was this woman and what did she believe? Why was I sitting there with her?

I never saw her again. Over the coming weeks, I gradually came to realize that this was a very important person, the main source of money for what was then a nascent Nazi movement in America. At the time, the whole thing seemed ridiculous. Today, not so much.

I never had a Nazi professor, never heard a Nazi media commentator, never read a mainstream book promoting Nazism. Until recently, such a bloodthirsty political longing has had to live in dark corners or come in beautifully deceptive packages such as this woman. For this reason, it has mostly escaped the notice of several generations. That doesn't mean it is not a danger to rationality, decency, and freedom. And it doesn't mean that it cannot grow and infect the ideological outlook of a new generation.

Another 20 years would go by before I seriously began to study and learn about this warped and freaky branch of totalitarian thought which today goes by many names (fascism, alt-right, neoreaction, and so on). I've learned that Nazism was and is the culmination of dangerous ideological tendencies from a century earlier. They didn't die after the war.

As Ludwig von Mises (one of the most consistent anti-Nazi intellectuals of the 20th century) warned repeatedly: bad ideas are never entirely gone; they come back and back, which is why the friends of liberty must never rest in learning about them and being true champions of the free society.

Over time, I've also learned that it is not enough to hate the left, or even to hate the government as it is (occupied or not). It is all about what we love. If we can identify and describe what we love, and with a clean conscience and sincere hope for the good of ourselves and everyone, we are where we need to be to recognize and resist all threats to liberty, from whatever source, beautiful or not.

As for my lunch partner that day, I assume that she is gone from this earth by now. But her ideological children are more numerous than ever.

II
THE POLITICS

The New Revanchism

The vast gulf that separates activist politics from real life seems to be growing.

If you listen to the leading politicians talk these days, you would think that the whole of American life is currently dominated by violence, injustice, discrimination, pillaging, isolation, deceit, fear, poverty, suffering, and decline generally. There are left and right wing versions of this story, but each portray a population cowering in fear, seething with resentment, obsessed with inequity, longing for a time gone by... and begging politicians for the strength and vision to change things.

It illustrates how it is that states thrive in bad times more than good, and how even a slight downtick in the rate of economic growth can enliven politicians to advertise their services to people clamoring for answers.

And in the US of 2016, once we turn off the media and shut down their voices, we discover a different reality all around us: more choice, more convenience, more peace, and new technologies and options that make life ever more wonderful. Because markets are still working and human ingenuity has not been entirely shut down by regulatory controls and taxes, we still see beauty all around us; so much so that you barely recognize the world that politicians describe.

It's truly bizarre, this disconnect. And what strikes you most about the world today is precisely how little confidence people have in political solutions. Indeed, they are mostly not buying what the politicians are selling. It's no wonder that roughly two thirds of Americans tell pollsters that they are both dissatisfied and alarmed at mainstream political options, and one in four are willing to say that they dislike both leading candidates.

If you feel the same, consider that you are in the majority.

Dystopia vs. Utopia

This strange disjunction struck me this Saturday. That afternoon, I finally bit the bullet and listened to Donald Trump's grimly dystopian nomination speech at the Republican convention. It was more dark than even I expected, and I'm writing as the guy who called him out for his brown-shirted fascist themes more than a year ago. He shouted at length about the state of country, how it is being invaded by parasites and criminals and how order is breaking down everywhere.

And this week, from the Democrats, we'll get a different dystopian view in which average people are people pillaged by the 1% and how billionaires are robbing us, while minority populations are suffering egregious exploitation and public institutions are being starved of money thanks to the selfishness of average people who are undertaxed and underregulated.

In both scenarios, nothing is working. Solutions are all about restoring some glorious past that somehow slipped away.

And yet, one recent Saturday evening, I went fact-finding in downtown Atlanta, Georgia, one of the world's most multicultural cities, just to see what the suffering masses were doing. What I found was a bustling, happily integrated, and busy community of consumers who were loving life. There were some large conventions taking place in town, with tens of thousands of people having come from all over the world to enjoy the nightlife in this city that is "too busy to hate."

People of all races, nationalities, languages, classes, and backgrounds populated the hotels, bars, restaurants, and streets. There were smiles all around. Street musicians played and their instrument cases filled with money tossed in by passersby. Students walked in packs. Professionals from all nations took in the sights. Every manner of fashion was on display.

The Hard Rock Cafe had a wait to get in. Hooters was doing crazy business. Every bar was standing-room only. A posh art-deco hotel with a fabulous bar was keeping its highly trained bartenders busy with fashionable cocktails, under a techy steel canopy that must have been amazing in the 1920s but still has that aspirational modern feel. Just to enter the bar on the 72nd floor of the Westin hotel required a 30-minute wait, and the people in the place delighted at the bird's eye view of this spectacular city. In a delightful touch, the room rotated slowly in circles to show off the achievement of human hands.

People at the bar were taking food and drink selfies and posting them in Snapchat and Instagram and gossiping among themselves about the people who liked or failed to like their posts. They commented on the music selections, how they love this singer and band and don't like this singer and band. They posted their comments on their dozens of social accounts from their smartphones, each one of which had been customized for global and instant communication based on their own preferences.

Everywhere indoors and outdoors, you saw people walking briskly with their smartphones pointed forward, playing—you guessed it— Pokémon GO. Here is a game that has united humanity to a greater extent than every existing political establishment.

Where was the violent crime? I didn't see any. There was no feeling of threat. Also, I didn't see any police presence. Remarkably, the teeming masses seemed to be managing themselves just fine. People were laughing, talking, walking, delighting in the sights and sounds, falling in love, and generally doing what people do in real life.

What Makes this Place Work?

Now, if you were visiting from another planet, you would most certainly discover this scene, pronounce it to be working beautifully, and then ask the question: why? There is one common element here: commerce. Every behavior, every action, was knitted together by the market operating at full capacity. Every institution used cash as the accounting nexus to determine its success or failure. This is true of the drivers (thank you ridesharing!), the food-servers, the shops, the condos, the hotels, everything. There is no plan, no script. And yet everywhere you look in this great city, you see the working energy of commerce and private enterprise, each instance of private property employed in the service of the one and the many.

To be sure, all these people pay taxes. Every business obeys regulations. Annoying things like zoning still exist. But the question is: are these interventions in the market order the thing that makes this beautiful community work? Or do they drag it down and slow its operations?

Even a casual observer knows the answer. Commerce is what creates this evolving community of mutual interest. Commerce is the heart of this system. It is because of commerce that the divisions created by political agitation are nowhere in evidence. It is because of commerce that people put aside race, class, gender, and even language, and instead discover value and dignity in people as people. And the city here is playing its traditional role of bringing hugely different people together in a common and coordinated effort to build a more wonderful life.

For this to exist in Atlanta is particularly impressive. This is a city that has been destroyed multiple times, mostly by various forms of political intervention, extending from General Sherman's fires in the latter days of the Civil War all the way through to the urban planning of the 1960s and 1970s. What a blessed relief when governments finally gave up the business of trying to make this city into something of their own design and learned to just let it be what it wanted to be. This is the reason for Atlanta's beautiful revival over the last 20 years.

Whither the State

If you think about it, we are depending on the state ever less. Sure, people are glad to take their food stamps and other benefits when necessary. But on a practical level, the state does very little for us as compared with the past. The loss of control by politics is palpable. The state has lost ground in communications, transportation, security provision, education, consumer protection, and cross-border dealings, and can no longer expect anything like a unified acquiescence to any aspect of its rule.

Globally, poverty and hunger are in dramatic decline, not because of government aid and planning, but because of private-sector innovation and ever-more intricate trade relationships. More human beings experience what it is like to possess human rights than at any time in history, and this is not due to bureaucracies and agencies but to the spread of markets, communications, and economic efficiencies.

Where does that leave the great statist project? No matter what the state does today, there will be a cross-section of the population screaming for it to stop. Even in once-nonnegotiable sectors like money production, there is now competition with the traditional public-sector monopoly.

A century ago, this thing called the state bragged that it would manage the whole of our lives better than we could manage them ourselves. We look around and everywhere we see failure in the very things it aspired to do. And when we look for successes, we see only the beauty of private enterprise in a digital age.

The Politics of Revanchism

If your life were devoted to power, to the well-being of the public sector, to the thriving of bureaucracy, to holding a people captive to a civic religion, how are our times going to make you feel? The overwhelming sense is that you and your cause have lost territory that you once owned and controlled. Much of it is already gone. Much more of it is going fast.

In late 19th century France following the Franco-Prussian war, a group of reactionaries determined to recapture lost lands formed a movement: Revanchism, from the French term for revenge. They swore they would get it all back. They would avenge their losses. The movement came to be characterized by hatred, bitterness that comes with loss, and a loathing of modernity, dedicated to stopping the forward flow of progress.

This is more and more the basis of modern politics and its attitude toward people and technology today. How dare people move on without political management! How dare they push forward with building their petty lives while ignoring the doctrines of the civic religion and paying obeisance to the masters who rule the social order!

Revanchism in our time has both left-wing and right-wing forms.

The left seethes at concentrated wealth, peer-to-peer technology, homeschooling, gun buyers who provide their own security, members of the bourgeoisie who have lost interest in their fanatical dreams for perfect equality and social justice, and the customized, privatized, media-driven civilizations the youth have created for themselves in the online world.

The right rails against people who reject nationalism, dare to live different lifestyles, doubt the glories of the latest political messiah, question authority of all types, defy the cops, live and love how they want, outsource business and buys abroad, while it tolerates things once heretical and keep disrupting the status quo by finding ways to innovate around incumbent industries and ruling-class elites.

What the left and right share in common is a demand to go back, to reclaim, to seek revenge against those who resist them. They want it all back: communications, education, technology, transportation, consumer protection, and the whole of the service economy that is governed by the private, spontaneous, innovative, and personalized app economy.

Today's political establishment fails to understand the way modern life works. They aren't just fuddy duddies. They are angry reactionaries, generals of revanchist armies, each bearing a distinct color, and their cry is to restore the *status quo ante*.

Take a look at any bustling city center and observe how people truly live. Here is the future. There is no going back.

Trumpism: The Ideology

In early 2015, Donald Trump was a crank and joke, living proof that making lots of money doesn't mean you have the answers, and further proof that being a capitalist doesn't mean you necessarily like or understand capitalism. His dabbling in politics was widely regarded as a silly distraction.

By late summer of the same year, he led the polls among the pack of Republican aspirants to the office of President of the United States. While all the other candidates were following the rules, playing the media, saying the right things, obeying the civic conventions, Trump took the opposite approach. He didn't care. He said whatever. Tens of thousands gathered at his rallies to thrill to the moment.

Suddenly he was serious, if only for a time, and hence it became time to take his political worldview seriously.

I heard Trump speak live at FreedomFest in July 2015, my first exposure to his worldview. The speech lasted an hour, and my jaw was on the floor most of the time. I had never before witnessed such a brazen display of nativistic jingoism, along with a complete disregard for economic reality. It was an awesome experience, a perfect repudiation of all good sense and intellectual sobriety.

Yes, he was against the establishment, against existing conventions. It also served as an important reminder: as bad as the status quo is, it could be worse. Trump, it seemed clear to me, was dedicated to taking us there.

His speech was like an interwar séance of once-powerful dictators who inspired multitudes, drove countries into the ground, and died grim deaths. I kept thinking of books like John T. Flynn's *As We Go Marching*, especially Chapter Ten that so brilliantly chronicles a form of statism that swept Europe in the 1930s. It grew up in the firmament of failed economies, cultural upheaval, and social instability, and it lives by stoking the fires of bourgeois resentment.

Since World War II, the ideology he represents has usually lived in dark corners, and we don't even have a name for it anymore. The right name, the correct name, the historically accurate name, is fascism. I don't use that word as an insult only. It is accurate.

Though hardly anyone talks about it today, we really should. It is still real. It exists. It is distinct. It is not going away. Trump has tapped into it, absorbing unto his own political ambitions every conceivable resentment (race, class, sex, religion, economic) and promising a new order of things under his mighty hand.

You would have to be hopelessly ignorant of modern history not to see the outlines and where they end up. I want to laugh about what he said, like reading a comic-book version of Franco, Mussolini, or Hitler. And truly I did laugh as he denounced the existence of tech support in India that serves American companies ("how can it be cheaper to call people there than here?"—as if he still thinks that long-distance charges apply). But in politics, history shows that laughter can turn too quickly to tears.

So, what does Trump actually believe? He does have a philosophy, though it takes a bit of insight and historical understanding to discern it. Of course, race baiting is essential to the ideology, and there was plenty of that. When a Hispanic man asked a question, Trump interrupted him and asked if he had been sent by the Mexican government. He took it a step further, dividing blacks from Hispanics by inviting a black man to the microphone to tell how his own son was killed by an illegal immigrant.

Because Trump is the only one who speaks this way, he can count on support from the darkest elements of American life. He doesn't need to actually advocate racial homogeneity, call for whites-only signs to be hung at immigration control, or push for expulsion or extermination of undesirables. Because such views are verboten, he has the field alone, and he can count on the support of those who think that way by making the right noises.

Trump also tosses little bones to the religious right, enough to allow them to believe that he represents their interests. Yes, it's implausible and hilarious. At the speech I heard, he pointed out further than he is a Presbyterian, and thus he is personally affected every time ISIS beheads a Christian.

But as much as racial and religious resentment is part of his rhetorical apparatus, it is not his core. His core is about business, his own business and his acumen thereof. He is living proof that being a successful capitalist is no predictor of one's appreciation for an actual free market (stealing not trading is more his style). It only implies a love of money and a longing for the power that comes with it. Trump has both.

What do capitalists on his level do? They beat the competition. What does he believe he should do as president? Beat the competition, which means other countries, which means wage a trade war. If you listen to him, you would suppose that the United States is in some sort of massive, epochal struggle for supremacy with China, India, Malaysia, and, pretty much everyone else in the world.

It takes a bit to figure out what this could mean. He speaks of the United States as if it were one thing, one single firm. A business. "We" are in competition with "them," as if the country was IBM competing against Samsung, Apple, or Dell. "We" are not 300 million people pursuing unique dreams and ideas, with special tastes or interests, cooperating with people around the world to build prosperity. "We" are doing one thing, and that is being part of one business.

In effect, he believes that he is running to be the CEO of the country—not just of the government. He is often compared with Ross Perot, another wealthy businessman who made an independent run. But Perot only promised to bring business standards to government. Trump wants to run the entire nation as if it were Trump Tower.

In this capacity, he believes that he will make deals with other countries that cause the United States to come out on top, whatever that could mean. He conjures up visions of himself or one of his associates sitting across the table from some Indian or Chinese leader and making wild demands that they will buy such and such amount of product, or else "we" won't buy "their" product. He fantasizes about placing phone calls to "Saudi Arabia," the country, and telling "it" what he thinks about oil prices.

Trade theory developed over hundreds of years plays no role in his thinking at all. To him, America is a homogenous unit, no different from his own business enterprise. With his run for president, he is really making a takeover bid, not just for another company to own but for an entire country to manage from the top down, under his proven and brilliant record of business negotiation and acquisition.

You see why the whole speech came across as bizarre? It was. And yet, maybe it was not. In the 18th century, there is a trade theory called mercantilism that posited something similar: Ship the goods out and keep the money in. It builds up industrial cartels that live at the expense of the consumer.

In the 19th century, this penchant for industrial protectionism and mercantilism became guild socialism, which mutated later into fascism and then into Nazism. You can read Mises to find out more on how this works.

What's distinct about Trumpism, and the tradition of thought it represents, is that it is not leftist in its cultural and political outlook (see how he is praised for rejecting "political correctness"), and yet still totalitarian in the sense that it seeks total control of society and economy and demands no limits on state power.

Whereas the left has long attacked bourgeois institutions like family, church, and property, fascism has made its peace with all three. It (very wisely) seeks political strategies that call on the organic matter of the social structure and inspire masses of people to rally around the nation as a personified ideal in history, under the leadership of a great and highly accomplished man.

Trump believes himself to be that man. He sounds fresh, exciting, even thrilling, like a man with a plan and a complete disregard for the existing establishment and all its weakness and corruption.

This is how strongmen take over countries. They say some true things, boldly, and conjure up visions of national greatness under their leadership. They've got the flags, the music, the hype, the hysteria, the resources, and they work to extract that thing in many people that seeks heroes and momentous struggles in which they can prove their greatness.

Think of Commodus (161–192 AD) in his war against the corrupt Roman senate. His ascension to power came with the promise of renewed Rome. What he brought was inflation, stagnation, and suffering. Historians have usually dated the fall of Rome from his leadership.

Or, if you prefer pop culture, think of Bane, the would-be dictator of Gotham in Batman, who promises an end to democratic corruption, weakness, and loss of civic pride. He sought a revolution against the prevailing elites in order to gain total power unto himself.

These people are all the same. They purport to be populists, while loathing the decisions people actually make in the marketplace (such as buying Chinese goods or hiring Mexican employees).

Oh how they love the people, and how they hate the establishment. They defy all civic conventions. Their ideology is somehow organic to the nation, not a wacky import like socialism. They promise a new era based on pride, strength, heroism, triumph. They have an obsession with the problem of trade and mercantilist belligerence at the only solution. They have zero conception of the social order as a complex and extended ordering of individual plans, one that functions through freedom.

This is a dark history, and I seriously doubt that Trump himself is aware of it. Instead, he just makes it up as he goes along, speaking from his gut, just like Uncle Harry at Thanksgiving dinner, just like two guys at the bar during last call.

This penchant has always served him well. It cannot serve a whole nation well. Indeed, the very prospect is terrifying, and not just for the immigrant groups and foreign peoples he has chosen to scapegoat for all the country's problems. It's a disaster in waiting for everyone.

My own prediction is that the political exotica he represents will not last. It's a moment in time. The thousands who attend his rallies and scream their heads off will head home, and return to enjoying movies, smartphones, and mobile apps from all over the world, partaking in the highest standard of living experienced in the whole of human history, granted courtesy of the global market economy in which no one rules. We will not go back.

Waking Up to the Reality of Fascism

Donald Trump has been on a roll, breaking new ground in uses for state power.

Closing the internet? Sure. "We have to see Bill Gates and a lot of different people... We have to talk to them about, maybe in certain areas, closing that Internet up in some ways."

Registering Muslims? Lots of people thought he misspoke. But he laterclarified: "There should be a lot of systems, beyond databases. We should have a lot of systems."

Why not just bar all Muslims at the border? Indeed, and to the massive cheers of his supporters, Trump has called for the "total and complete shutdown of Muslims entering the United States."

Internment camps? Trump cites the FDR precedent: Italians, Germans, and Japanese "couldn't go five miles from their homes. They weren't allowed to use radios, flashlights. I mean, you know, take a look at what FDR did many years ago and he's one of the most highly respected presidents."

Rounding up millions of people? He'll create a "deportation force" to hunt down and remove 11 million illegal immigrants.

Killing wives and children? That too. "When you get these terrorists, you have to take out their families."

Political Vocabulary

This litany of ideas has finally prompted mainstream recognition of the incredibly obvious: If Donald Trump has an ideology, it is best described as fascism.

Even Republican commentators, worried that he might be unstoppable, are saying it now. Military historian and Marco Rubio adviser Max Boot tweeted that "Trump is a fascist. And that's not a term I use loosely or often. But he's earned it." Bush adviser John Noonan said the same.

The mainstream press is more overt. CNN's Chris Cuomo asked Trump point blank if he is a fascist. The Atlantic writes: "It's hard to remember a time when a supposedly mainstream candidate had no interest in differentiating ideas he's endorsed from those of the Nazis."

There is a feeling of shock in the air, but anyone paying attention should have seen the summer of 2015. Why did it take so long for the consciousness to dawn?

The word fascism has been used too often in political discourse, and almost always imprecisely. It's a bit like the boy who cried wolf. You warn about wolves so much that no one takes you seriously when a real one actually shows up.

Lefties since the late 1930s have tended to call non-leftists fascists—which has led to a discrediting of the word itself. As time went on, the word became nothing but a vacuous political insult. It's what people say about someone with whom they disagree. It doesn't mean much more than that.

Then in the 1990s came Godwin's Law: "As an online discussion grows longer, the probability of a comparison involving Nazis or Hitler approaches 100 percent." This law provided a convenient way to dismiss all talk of fascism as Internet babblings deployed in the midst of flame wars.

Godwin's Law made worse the perception that followed the end of

World War II: that fascism was a temporary weird thing that afflicted a few countries but had been vanquished from the earth thanks to the Allied war victory. It would no longer be a real problem but rather a swear word with no real substance.

Fascism Is Real

Without the term fascism as an authentic descriptor, we have a problem. We have no accurate way to identify what is in fact the most politically successful movement of the 20th century. It is a movement that still exists today, because the conditions that gave rise to it are unchanged.

The whole burden of one of the most famous pro-freedom books of the century—Hayek's *The Road to Serfdom*—was to warn that fascism was a more immediate and pressing danger to the developed world than Russian-style socialism. And this is for a reason: Hayek said that "brown" fascism did not represent a polar opposite of "red" socialism. In the interwar period, it was common to see both intellectuals and politicians move fluidly from one to the other.

"The rise of Fascism and Nazism was not a reaction against the socialist trends of the preceding period," wrote Hayek, "but a necessary outcome of those tendencies."

In Hayek's reading, the dynamic works like this. The socialists build the state machinery, but their plans fail. A crisis arrives. The population seeks answers. Politicians claiming to be anti-socialist step up with new authoritarian plans that purport to reverse the problem. Their populist appeal taps into the lowest political instincts (nativism, racism, religious bigotry, and so on) and promises a new order of things under better, more efficient rule.

Last July, I heard Trump speak, and his talk displayed all the features of fascist rhetoric. He began with trade protectionism and held up autarky as an ideal. He moved to immigration, leading the crowd to believe that all their economic and security troubles were due to

dangerous foreign elements among us. Then came the racial dog whistles: Trump demanded of a Hispanic questioner whether he was a
plant sent by the government of Mexico.

There was more. He railed against the establishment that is
incompetent and lacking in energy. He bragged about his lack of
interest-group ties—which is another way of saying that only he can
become the purest sort of dictator, with no quid pro quos to tie him
down.

Trump is clearly not pushing himself as a traditional American
president, heading an executive branch and working with Congress
and the judicial branch. He imagines himself as running to head a personal state: his will would be the one will for the country. He has no
real plans beyond putting himself in charge—not only of the government but, he imagines, the entire country. It's a difference of substance
that is very serious.

The rest of the campaign has been easy to predict. He refashioned
himself as pro-family, anti-PC, and even pro-religion. These traits
come with the package—both a reaction to the far left and a fulfill-
ment of its centralist ambitions.

The key to understanding fascism is this: It preserves the despotic
ambitions of socialism while removing its most politically unpopular
elements. In an atmosphere of fear and loathing, it assures the population that it can keep its property, religion, and faith—provided all
these elements are channeled into a grand national project under a
charismatic leader of high competence.

Douthat's Analysis

As the realization has spread that Trump is the real deal, so
has the quality of reflection on its implication. Most impressive so
far has been Ross Douthat'sarticle in the *New York Times*. As he
explains, Trump displays as least seven features of Umberto Eco's list
of fascist traits:

A cult of action, a celebration of aggressive mascu-
linity, an intolerance of criticism, a fear of difference
and outsiders, a pitch to the frustrations of the lower
middle class, an intense nationalism and resentment
at national humiliation, and a "popular elitism" that
promises every citizen that they're part of "the best
people of the world."

In this, Trump is different from other American politicians who
have been called fascist, writes Douthat. George Wallace was a local-
rights guy and hated Washington, whereas Trump loves power and
thinks only in terms of centralization. Pat Buchanan's extreme nativism was always tempered by his attachment to Catholic moral teaching
that puts brakes on power ambitions.

Ross Perot was called a fascist, but actually he was a government
reformer who wanted to bring business standards to government
finance, which is very different from wanting to manage the entire
country. And, for all his nonsense about jobs going to Mexico, Perot
generally avoided racialist dog whistles.

Why Now and Not Before?

Why has genuine fascism been kept at bay in America? Why has
the American right never taken the final step that might have plunged
it into authoritarian, nativist aspirations?

Here Douthat is especially insightful:

Part of the explanation has to be that the American
conservative tradition has always included important
elements—a libertarian skepticism of state power, a
stress on localism and states' rights, a religious and particularly Protestant emphasis on the conscience of an
individual over the power of the collective—that inoc-
ulated our politics against fascism's appeal.

Douthat singles out libertarianism as an ideological brake on fascist longings. This is precisely right. Libertarianism grows out of the liberal tradition, which is about far more than merely hating the ruling-class establishment. Classical liberalism has universalist longings, embodied in its defenses of free trade, free speech, free migration, and freedom of religion. The central-planning feature of fascistic ideology is absolutely ruled out by libertarian love for spontaneous social and economic forces at work in society.

As for "energy" emanating from the executive branch, the liberal tradition can't be clearer. No amount of intelligence, resources, or determined will from the top down can make government work. The problem is the apparatus itself, not the personalities and values of the rulers who happen to be in charge.

(I'm leaving aside the deep and bizarre irony that many self-professed libertarians have fallen for Trump, a fact which should be deeply embarrassing to anyone and everyone who has affection for human liberty. And good for Ron Paul for denouncing Trump's authoritarianism in no uncertain terms.)

Can He Win?

Douthat seriously doubts that Trump can finally win over Republicans, due to "his lack of any real religious faith, his un-libertarian style and record, his clear disdain for the ideas that motivate many of the most engaged Republicans."

I'm not so sure. The economic conditions that led to a rise of Hitler in Germany, Mussolini in Italy, and Franco in Spain are nowhere close to being replicated here. Even so, income growth has stagnated, middle-class social ambitions are frustrated, and many aspects of government services are failing (such as Obamacare). Add fear of terrorism to the mix, and the conditions, at least for some, are nearly right. What Trumpism represents is an attempt to address these problems through more of the same means that have failed in the past.

It's time to dust off that copy of *The Road to Serfdom* and realize that the biggest threats to liberty come from unexpected places. While the rank and file are worrying themselves about the influence of progressive professors and group identity politics, they need to open their eyes to the possibility that the gravest threat to American rights and liberties exists within their own ranks.

Two Flavors of Tyranny

Maybe you have noticed the strangely implausible similarities between the cobbled-together platforms of Bernie Sanders and Donald Trump. On the surface, they represent opposite extremes. But in their celebration of the nation state as the people's salvation—their burning calls to overthrow the existing elites and replace them with a more intense form of top-down rule—they have much in common.

Remember that the Nazis and Communists hated each other in the interwar period and, of course, fought each other to the bloody end in the war itself. After the Nazis lost control of the nations they conquered, the Communists swept in, trading one tyranny for another.

To imagine that these systems somehow represent polar opposites is bizarre. Both systems extolled the primacy of the state. Both practiced economic central planning. Both upheld the nation over the individual. Both created a cult of leadership. Both experiments in top-down social order ended in calamity and massive violations of human rights.

How could these two systems, so similar in operation, be so antagonistic? I guess you had to be there.

Back to the Past

Oddly, we are there now. When it comes to politics, it's the 1930s all over again—or at least an updated version.

We are actually living through a period in which the revolutionary

53

left and the revolutionary right have merged—fighting the establishment to make government bigger—in a way that is mostly lost on their respective supporters.

Sanders and Trump differ on particulars, though where exactly is not quite obvious. Yes, Trump is against gun control, and Sanders extols it. Sanders wants to pillage the rich, and Trump doesn't want to be pillaged. Sanders makes a big deal about global warming, and Trump doesn't seem to take it seriously.

But those are the tweaks and idiosyncrasies in an overarching system on which they both agree: the nation state as the central organizing unit of life itself. They have different priorities on who it should serve and where the state should expand most.

But they agree on the need to protect and enlarge state power. Neither accepts any principled limits on what the state may rightfully do to the individual. Even on big issues where one might think they disagree—healthcare, immigration, and control of lands by the federal government—their positions are largely indistinguishable.

And yet, they and their supporters loathe each other. Each considers the other an enemy to be destroyed. This is not a fight about power as such but about in whose service it will be used.

Most of their supporters don't see it that way, of course. They imagine themselves to be rebels fighting power itself, however they want to define it: Wall Street, the party establishment, the paid-off politicians, the bureaucracy, the billionaires, the foreigners, the special interests, and so on.

But notice that neither attacks government authority as such. Both aspire to use it and grow it for their purposes.

The Marketing of Control

Insight here is provided by F.A. Hayek in *The Road to Serfdom*, published in 1944 (another time when such issues were pressing), clarifying that the difference here is not in substance but style.

"The conflict between the Fascist or National-Socialist and the older socialist parties must indeed very largely be regarded as the kind of conflict which is bound to arise between rival socialist factions," he wrote. "There was no difference between them about the question of it being the will of the state which should assign to each person his proper place in society."

What is the difference? It was a matter of the demographics of political support and the differing classes in society that expected to benefit from a total state. The old socialists sought support from within working classes and depended heavily on the support of intellectuals.

The new form of socialists were supported by the young generation, "out of that contempt for profit-making fostered by socialist teaching." These people "spurned independent positions which involved risk, and flocked in ever-increasing numbers into salaried positions which promised security." They were demanding a place yielding them income and power to which their training entitled them but which seemed perpetually out of reach.

Though he was talking about 1930s Europe, it seems like a good description of Sanders supporters, who overwhelmingly come from the youngest voters. Betrayed by the educational system, stuck with a bleak job outlook, burdened with debt, trapped in a broken healthcare market, feeling like the system is rigged against them, they have turned to the politician who promises heaven on earth through the pillaging of the wealthy elites.

Then you have the fascist and national socialist right, with its own forms of scapegoating and its own class appeal. This approach says: your troubles are due to the outsiders, the immigrants, the media elite, the Muslims, the intellectuals and their political correctness.

The appeal, then as now, is a new form of identity politics based on nation and race. To them, the idea of equality is a mere cover for a power grab, a subversive trick to further the interests of the elites and nefarious "others."

Replace Failure with Failure

As Hayek reminds us, neither faction emerged in a vacuum. "Their tactics were developed in a world already dominated by socialist policy and the problems it creates." But instead of viewing the problem as statism itself, they push for state power to be used in a different way.

The *New York Times* reported that: "Iowa Republican caucusgoers are deeply unhappy with how the federal government is working," but, for some reason, many GOP voters have yet to figure out that the military, the surveillance state, and immigration control that they love are the government they claim to hate.

Last Gasps

Why pay attention to this circus at all? It's fascinating to watch the crackup of the old failed political order. It is happening to both parties and also to the public sector they scrabble to control. Their promise of better living through bigger bureaucracies has flopped.

Meanwhile, in our daily lives, the future is with borderless distributed technologies, managed not by zero-sum elections but by the digital marketplace. This is what is turning the world upside down.

Still, the political sector continues to exist, and becomes more unstable and ridiculous by the day. You can see this as tragic and terrible, or fun and delightful. I remind myself daily to choose the latter route.

Do You Know
What a Nation Is?

O n July 4, we celebrate something called the nation, but what is a nation? What is the source of our affections and loyalties?

We all assume that we know the answer to the question. But when you drill down, you find out that there is no clear agreement. In fact, disagreement on this vital issue is a huge source of division and political strife in the world today.

Divergent views on what constitutes nationhood is one aspect of why Trump's claims make sense to his followers but not to the editorial pages, why Elizabeth Warren's tirades strike some as sensible and others as silly, why some people regard the rise of the alt-right (or the antifa) as a saving grace and others see it as a sign of the end times.

Ask yourself: what do you believe a nation to be? Do you have a clear understanding of your own belief? Regardless of your politics, but especially if you consider yourself to be a libertarian, you need to get this settled.

In 1882, the great French historian Ernst Renan penned a passionate and brilliant essay on the question. Ludwig von Mises himself rallied around this essay as the best expression of classically liberal doctrine. If another essay has done as good a job in dealing with the issue, I'm unaware of it. He wrote it while the age of monarchy was coming to a close, as the rise of democracy was occurring everywhere. Ideologies like socialism, imperialism, and "scientific" racism were vying to replace old-world understandings of political community.

Even if you reject his final thesis—that the perception of nationhood is an affair of the heart and nothing else—you can still be challenged by his analysis.

Renan delineates five conventional theories of nationhood from history and practice.

Dynasty. This view believes that ruling-class lineage forms the foundation of nationhood. It's about a history of initial conquest by one family or tribe over one people, its struggle to gain and maintain power and legitimacy, its marriages, wars, treaties, and alliances, along with a heroic legend. This is a solid description of European experience in feudal times, but it is not necessary for nationhood.

The dynastic sense of what nationhood is has largely evaporated in the 20th century, and yet nationhood is still with us. Renan saw that the dynastic view of the nation is not a permanent feature of the concept but only incidental to a time and place, and wholly replaceable. "A nation can exist without a dynastic principle," writes Renan, "and even those nations which have been formed by dynasties can be separated from them without therefore ceasing to exist."

Religion. The belief that a nation needs to practice a single faith has been the basis of wars and killings since the beginning of recorded history. It seemed like nationhood couldn't exist without it, which is why the Schism of the 11th century and the Reformation of the 16th century led to such conflict.

Then emerged a beautiful idea: let people believe what they want to believe, so long as they are not hurting anyone. The idea was tried and it worked, and thus was born the idea of religious liberty that finally severed the idea of national belongingness from religious identity. Even as late as the 19th century, American political interests claimed that the US could not be a nation while accepting Catholic, Jewish, and Buddhist immigration. Today we see these claims for what they are, politically illicit longings for conquest over the right of conscience.

In addition, what might appear at first to be a single religion actually has radically different expressions. Pennsylvania Amish and Texas Baptists share the same religious designation but have vastly different praxis, and the same is true of Irish vs. Vietnamese vs. Guatemalan versions of Catholicism. This is also true of every other religious faith, including Judaism, Islam, and Hinduism. Overlooking this amounts to denying a persistent reality of all faiths in all times and places.

Race. In the second half of the 19th century, there arose the new science of race, which purported to explain the evolution of all human societies through a deterministic reduction to biological characteristics. It was concluded that only race is firm and fixed and the basis of belongingness. Renan grants that in the most primitive societies, race is a large factor. But then comes other more developed aspects of the human experience: language, religion, art, music, and commercial engagement that break down racial divisions and created a new basis for community. Focusing on race alone is a revanchist longing in any civilized society.

There is also a scientific problem too complex for simple resolution: no political community on earth can claim to be defined solely by racial identity because there is no pure race. This is why politics can never be reduced to ethnographic identity as a first principle. Racial ideology also trends toward the politics of violence: "No one has the right to go through the world fingering people's skulls, and taking them by the throat saying: 'You are of our blood; you belong to us!'"

Language. As with the other claims of what constitutes nationality, the claim of language unity has a superficial plausibility. Polyglot communities living under a unity state face constant struggles over schooling, official business, and other issues of speech. They have the feeling of being two or several nations, thus tempting people to believe that language itself is the basis of nationhood. But this actually makes little sense: the US, New Zealand, and the UK are not a single nation because they hold the same language in common. Latin America and Spain, Portugal and Brazil, share the same language but not the same nation.

There is also the issue that not even a single language is actually unified: infinite varieties of expression and dialect can cause ongoing confusion. How much, really, does the language of an urban native of New Jersey have to do with expressions used in rural Mississippi? "Language invites people to unite," writes Renan, "but it does not force them to do so." There is nothing mystically unifying about speaking the same language; language facilitates communication but does not forge a nation.

Geography. Natural boundaries are another case of nation-making in the past which, as with all these other principles, actually has little to do with permanent features of what really makes a nation. Rivers and mountains can be convenient ways to draw borders but they do not permanently shape political communities. Geography can be easily overcome. It is malleable, as American history shows. The existence of geographically non-contiguous nations further refutes the notion.

Americans speak of "sea to shining sea," but how does that make sense of Alaska and Hawaii? Also in the US, enclaves of past national loyalty are a feature of city life: little Brazil, Chinatown, little Havana, and so on. Even further, to try to force unity based on geography alone is very dangerous. "I know of no doctrine which is more arbitrary or more fatal," writes Renan, "for it allows one to justify any or every violence."

So What Is a Nation?

All the above have some plausible claim to explaining national attachment, but none hold up under close scrutiny.

Can we identify any single factor to account for people's sense of attachment to a political community?

In Renan's view, nationhood is a spiritual principle, a reflection of the affections we feel toward some kind of political community—its ideals, its past, its achievements, and its future. Where your heart is, there is your nation. This is why so many of us can feel genuine feelings of joy and even belongingness during July 4th celebrations. We are celebrating something in common: a feeling we have that we share with others, regardless of religion, race, language (this is, after all, a country where "Despacito" is the number one pop hit), geography, and even ideology.

It is all about affections of the heart, which appear without compulsion and exist prior to and far beyond any loyalties to a particular dynasty, regime, or anything else. And what is that source of inner pride Americans feel? It's about the way in which the American political experiment appears rooted in the freedom to have and to hold those affections, and ennobles them in American aspirations and institutions. As with any national experience, ours is a deeply flawed history but the love that we have in our hearts for the freedom that is the theme of this nation persists despite it all.

Renan has the last word: "Man is a slave neither of his race nor his language, nor of his religion, nor of the course of rivers nor of the direction taken by mountain chains. A large aggregate of men, healthy in mind and warm of heart, creates the kind of moral conscience which we call a nation."

The freedom of this moral conscience is what we celebrate when we feel pride in the American nation.

Why Is Trump Waging War on the Freedom Caucus?

W hy is Trump attacking the House Freedom Caucus? He has tweeted that "we must fight them."

My first thought: this is inevitable. Destiny is unfolding before our eyes!

There is the obvious fact that the Freedom Caucus was the reason the GOP's so-called replacement for Obamacare went down to defeat. They fought it for a solid reason: it would not have reduced premiums or deductibles, and it would not have increased access to a greater degree of choice in the health-insurance market.

These people knew this. How? Because there was not one word of that bill that enabled the health care industry to become more competitive. Competition is the standard by which reform must be judged. The core problem of Obamacare (among many) was that it froze the market in an artificial form and insulated it from competitive forces.

At minimum, any reform must unfreeze the market. The proposed reform did not do that.

Bad Reform

That means the reform would not have been good for the American people. It would not have been good for the Republican Party. And then the chance for real reform—long promised by many people in the party—would have been gone.

Trump latched on to the proposal without understanding it. Or, other theories: he doesn't care, he actually does favor universal coverage even if it is terrible, or he just wanted some pyrrhic victory even if it did nothing to improve the access.

The Freedom Caucus killed it. And I'm trying to think back in political history here, is there another time since World War II that a pro-freedom faction of the Republican Party killed a bill pushed by the majority that pertained to such a large sector and dealt with such a hugely important program?

I can't think of one.

What this signifies is extremely important. We might be see-ing the emergence of a classically liberal faction within the GOP, one that is self consciously driven by an agenda that is centered on a clear goal: getting us closer to an ideal of a free society. The Caucus isn't fully formed yet in an ideological sense, but its agenda is becoming less blurry by the day. (Andplease don't call them the "hard right wing.")

The old GOP coalition included nationalists, militarists, free enterprisers, and social conservatives. The Trump takeover has strained it to the breaking point. Now the genuine believers in freedom are gaining a better understanding of themselves and what they must do.

For the first times in our lives! Even in our parents' and grandpar-ents' lives!

The Larger Picture

Trump is obviously not a student of history or political philoso-phy, but he does embody a strain of thinking with a history that traces back in time. The tradition of thought he inhabits stands in radi-cal opposition to the liberal tradition. It always has. We just remain rather ignorant of this fact because the fascist tradition of thought has been dormant for many decades, and so is strangely unfamiliar to this generation of political obsSo let us be clear: this manner of think-ing that celebrates the nation-state, believes in great collectives on the move, panics about the demographic genocide of a race, rails against the "other" invading our shores, puts all hope in a powerful executive, and otherwise believes not in freedom but rather in compliance, loyalty, and hero worship—this manner of thinking has always and everywhere included liberals (or libertarians) as part of the enemy to be destroyed.

And why is this? Liberalism to them represents "rootless cosmopolitanism," in the old Nazi phrase. They are willing to do business with anyone, move anywhere, and imagine that the good life of peace and prosperity is more than enough to aspire to in order to achieve the best of all possible worlds. They don't believe that war is ennobling and heroic, but rather bloody and destructive. They are in awe of the creation of wealth out of simple exchanges and small innovations. They are champions of the old bourgeois spirit.

To the liberal mind, the goal of life is to live well in peace and experience social and financial gain, with ever more alleviation of life's pains and sufferings. Here is magic. Here is beauty. Here is true heroism.

The alt-right mind will have none of this. They want the clash, the war, the struggle against the enemy, big theaters of epic battles that pit great collectives against each other. If you want a hilarious caricature of this life outlook, no one does it better than Roderick Spode.

Natural Enemies

This is why these two groups can never get along politically. They desire different things. It has always and everywhere been true that when the strongmen of the right-Hegelian mindset gain control, they target the liberals for destruction. Liberals become the enemy that must be crushed.

And so it is that a mere few months into the presidency of this odd figure that the Freedom Caucus has emerged as a leading opposition. They will back him where they can but will otherwise adhere to the great principle of freedom. When their interests diverge, the Freedom

Caucus will go the other way. It is not loyalty but freedom that drives them. It is not party but principle that makes them do what they do.

To any aspiring despot, such views are intolerable, as bad as the reliable left-wing opposition.

Listen, I'm all for working with anyone to achieve freedom. When Trump is right (as he is on environmental regulation, capital gains taxes, and some other issues), he deserves to be backed. When he is wrong, he deserves to be opposed. This is not about partisanship. It is about obtaining freer lives.

But let us not languish in naïvete. The mindset of the right-wing Hegelian is not at all the same as a descendant of the legacy of Adam Smith. They know it. We need to know it too.

III

THE HISTORY

Policy Science Kills

The climate-change debate has many people wondering whether we should really turn over public policy—which deals with fundamental matters of human freedom—to a state-appointed scientific establishment. Must moral imperatives give way to the judgment of technical experts in the natural sciences? Should we trust their authority? Their power?

There is a real history here to consult. The integration of government policy and scientific establishments has reinforced bad science and yielded ghastly policies.

There's no better case study than the use of eugenics: the science, so called, of breeding a better race of human beings. It was popular in the Progressive Era and following, and it heavily informed US government policy. Back then, the scientific consensus was all in for public policy founded on high claims of perfect knowledge based on expert research. There was a cultural atmosphere of panic ("race suicide!") and a clamor for the experts to put together a plan to deal with it. That plan included segregation, sterilization, andlabor-market exclusion of the "unfit."

Ironically, climatology had something to do with it. Harvard professor Robert DeCourcy Ward (1867–1931) is credited with holding the first chair of climatology in the United States. He was a consummate member of the academic establishment. He was editor of the *American Meteorological Journal*, president of the Association of

American Geographers, and a member of both the American Academy of Arts and Sciences and the Royal Meteorological Society of London.

He also had an avocation. He was a founder of the American Restriction League. It was one of the first organizations to advocate reversing the traditional American policy of free immigration and replacing it with a "scientific" approach rooted in Darwinian evolutionary theory and the policy of eugenics. Centered in Boston, the league eventually expanded to New York, Chicago, and San Francisco. Its science inspired a dramatic change in US policy over labor law, marriage policy, city planning, and, its greatest achievements, the 1921 Emergency Quota Act and the 1924 Immigration Act. These were the first-ever legislated limits on the number of immigrants who could come to the United States.

Nothing Left to Chance

"Darwin and his followers laid the foundation of the science of eugenics," Ward alleged in his manifesto published in the *North American Review* in July 1910. "They have shown us the methods and possibilities of the product of new species of plants and animals.... In fact, artificial selection has been applied to almost every living thing with which man has close relations except man himself."

"Why," Ward demanded, "should the breeding of man, the most important animal of all, alone be left to chance?"

By "chance," of course, he meant *choice*.

"Chance" is how the scientific establishment of the Progressive Era regarded the free society. Freedom was considered to be unplanned, anarchic, chaotic, and potentially deadly for the race. To the Progressives, freedom needed to be replaced by a planned society administered by experts in their fields. It would be another 100 years before climatologists themselves became part of the policy-planning apparatus of the state, so Professor Ward busied himself in racial science and the advocacy of immigration restrictions.

Ward explained that the United States had a "remarkably favorable opportunity for practising eugenic principles." And there was a desperate need to do so, because "already we have no hundreds of thousands, but millions of Italians and Slavs and Jews whose blood is going into the new American race." This trend could cause Anglo-Saxon America to "disappear." Without eugenic policy, the "new American race" will not be a "better, stronger, more intelligent race" but rather a "weak and possibly degenerate mongrel."

Citing a report from the New York Immigration Commission, Ward was particularly worried about mixing American Anglo-Saxon blood with "long-headed Sicilians and those of the round-headed east European Hebrews."

Keep Them Out

"We certainly ought to begin at once to segregate, far more than we now do, all our native and foreign-born population which is unfit for parenthood," Ward wrote. "They must be prevented from breeding."

But even more effective, Ward wrote, would be strict quotas on immigration. While "our surgeons are doing a wonderful work," he wrote, they can't keep up in filtering out people with physical and mental disabilities pouring into the country and diluting the racial stock of Americans, turning us into "degenerate mongrels."

Such were the policies dictated by eugenic science, which, far from being seen as quackery from the fringe, was in the mainstream of academic opinion. President Woodrow Wilson, America's first professorial president, embraced eugenic policy. So did Supreme Court Justice Oliver Wendell Holmes Jr., who, in upholding Virginia's sterilization law, wrote, "Three generations of imbeciles are enough."

Looking through the literature of the era, I am struck by the near absence of dissenting voices on the topic. Popular books advocating eugenics and white supremacy, such as *The Passing of the Great Race* by Madison Grant, became immediate bestsellers. The opinions in these books—which are not for the faint of heart—were expressed long before the Nazis discredited such policies. They reflect the thinking of an entire generation, and are much more frank than one would expect to read now.

It's crucial to understand that all these opinions were not just about pushing racism as an aesthetic or personal preference. Eugenics was about politics: using the state to plan the population. It should not be surprising, then, that the entire anti-immigration movement was steeped in eugenics ideology. Indeed, the more I look into this history, the less I am able to separate the anti-immigrant movement of the Progressive Era from white supremacy in its rawest form.

Shortly after Ward's article appeared, the climatologist called on his friends to influence legislation. Restriction League president Prescott Hall and Charles Davenport of the Eugenics Record Office began the effort to pass a new law with specific eugenic intent. It sought to limit the immigration of southern Italians and Jews in particular. And immigration from Eastern Europe, Italy, and Asia did indeed plummet.

The Politics of Eugenics

Immigration wasn't the only policy affected by eugenic ideology. Edwin Black's *War Against the Weak: Eugenics and America's Campaign to Create a Master Race* (2003, 2012) documents how eugenics was central to Progressive Era politics. An entire generation of academics, politicians, and philanthropists used bad science to plot the extermination of undesirables. Laws requiring sterilization claimed 60,000 victims. Given the attitudes of the time, it's surprising that the carnage in the United States was so low. Europe, however, was not as fortunate.

Eugenics became part of the standard curriculum in biology, with William Castle's 1916 *Genetics and Eugenics* commonly used for over 15 years, with four iterative editions.

Literature and the arts were not immune. John Carey's *The Intellectuals and the Masses: Pride and Prejudice Among the Literary Intelligentsia, 1880–1939* (2005) shows how the eugenics mania affected the entire modernist literary movement of the United Kingdom, with such famed minds as T.S. Eliot and D.H. Lawrence getting wrapped up in it.

Economics Gets In on the Act

Remarkably, even economists fell under the sway of eugenic pseudoscience. Thomas Leonard's explosively brilliant *Illiberal Reformers: Race, Eugenics, and American Economics in the Progressive Era* (2016) documents in excruciating detail how eugenic ideology corrupted the entire economics profession in the first two decades of the 20th century. Across the board, in the books and articles of the profession, you find all the usual concerns about race suicide, the poisoning of the national bloodstream by inferiors, and the desperate need for state planning to breed people the way ranchers breed animals. Here we find the template for the first-ever large-scale implementation of scientific social and economic policy.

Students of the history of economic thought will recognize the names of these advocates: Richard T. Ely, John R. Commons, Irving Fisher, Henry Rogers Seager, Arthur N. Holcombe, Simon Patten, John Bates Clark, Edwin R.A. Seligman, and Frank Taussig. They were the leading members of the professional associations, the editors of journals, and the high-prestige faculty members of the top universities. It was a given among these men that classical political economy had to be rejected. There was a strong element of self-interest at work. As Leonard puts it, "laissez-faire was inimical to economic expertise and thus an impediment to the vocational imperatives of American economics."

Irving Fisher, whom Joseph Schumpeter described as "the greatest economist the United States has ever produced" (an assessment later repeated by Milton Friedman), urged Americans to "make of eugenics a religion."

Speaking at the Race Betterment Conference in 1915, Fisher said eugenics was "the foremost plan of human redemption." The American Economic Association (which is still today the most prestigious trade association of economists) published openly racist tracts such as the chilling *Race Traits and Tendencies of the American Negro* by Frederick Hoffman. It was a blueprint for the segregation, exclusion, dehumanization, and eventual extermination of the black race.

Hoffman's book called American blacks "lazy, thriftless, and unreliable," and well on their way to a condition of "total depravity and utter worthlessness." Hoffman contrasted them with the "Aryan race," which is "possessed of all the essential characteristics that make for success in the struggle for the higher life."

Even as Jim Crow restrictions were tightening against blacks, and the full weight of state power was being deployed to wreck their economic prospects, the American Economic Association's tract said that the white race "will not hesitate to make war upon those races who prove themselves useless factors in the progress of mankind."

Richard T. Ely, a founder of the American Economic Association, advocated segregation of nonwhites (he seemed to have a special loathing of the Chinese) and state measures to prohibit their propagation. He took issue with the very "existence of these feeble persons." He also supported state-mandated sterilization, segregation, and labor-market exclusion.

That such views were not considered shocking tells us so much about the intellectual climate of the time.

If your main concern is who is bearing whose children, and how many, it makes sense to focus on labor and income. Only the fit should be admitted to the workplace, the eugenicists argued. The unfit should be excluded so as to discourage their immigration and, once here, their propagation. This was theorigin of the minimum wage, a policy designed to erect a high wall to the "unemployables."

Women, Too

Another implication follows from eugenic policy: government must control women.

It must control their comings and goings. It must control their work hours—or whether they work at all. As Leonard documents, here we find the origin of the maximum-hour workweek and many other interventions against the free market. Women had been pouring into the workforce for the last quarter of the 19th century, gaining the economic power to make their own choices. Minimum wages, maximum hours, safety regulations, and so on passed in state after state during the first two decades of the 20th century and were carefully targeted to exclude women from the workforce. The purpose was to control contact, manage breeding, and reserve the use of women's bodies for the production of the master race.

Leonard explains:

> American labor reformers found eugenic dangers nearly everywhere women worked, from urban piers to home kitchens, from the tenement block to the respectable lodging house, and from factory floors to leafy college campuses. The privileged alumna, the middle-class boarder, and the factory girl were all accused of threatening Americans' racial health.
>
> Paternalists pointed to women's health. Social purity moralists worried about women's sexual virtue. Family-wage proponents wanted to protect men from the economic competition of women. Maternalists warned that employment was incompatible with motherhood. Eugenicists feared for the health of the race.
>
> "Motley and contradictory as they were," Leonard

adds, "all these progressive justifications for regulating the employment of women shared two things in common. They were directed at women only. And they were designed to remove at least some women from employment."

The Lesson We Haven't Learned

Today we find eugenic aspirations to be appalling. We rightly value the freedom of association. We understand that permitting people free choice over reproductive decisions does not threaten racial suicide but rather points to the strength of a social and economic system. We don't want scientists using the state to cobble together a master race at the expense of freedom. For the most part, we trust the "invisible hand" to govern demographic trajectories, and we recoil at those who don't.

But back then, eugenic ideology was conventional scientific wisdom, and hardly ever questioned except by a handful of old-fashioned advocates of laissez-faire. The eugenicists' books sold in the millions, and their concerns became primary in the public mind. Dissenting scientists—and there were some—were excluded by the profession and dismissed as cranks attached to a bygone era.

Eugenic views had a monstrous influence over government policy, and they ended free association in labor, marriage, and migration. Indeed, the more you look at this history, the more it becomes clear that white supremacy, misogyny, and eugenic pseudoscience were the intellectual foundations of modern statecraft.

Why is there so little public knowledge of this period and the motivations behind its progress? Why has it taken so long for scholars to blow the lid off this history of racism, misogyny, and the state?

The partisans of the state regulation of society have no reason to talk about it, and today's successors of the Progressive Movement and its eugenic views want to distance themselves from the past as much as possible. The result has been a conspiracy of silence.

There are, however, lessons to be learned. When you hear of some impending crisis that can only be solved by scientists working with public officials to force people into a new pattern that is contrary to their free will, there is reason to raise an eyebrow. Science is a process of discovery, not an end state, and its consensus of the moment should not be enshrined in the law and imposed at gunpoint.

We've been there and done that, and the world is rightly repulsed by the results.

Why the Holocaust
Should Matter to You

People tour the nation's capital to be delighted by symbols of America's greatness and history. They seek out monuments and museums that pay tribute to the nation state and its works. They want to think about the epic struggles of the past, and how mighty leaders confronted and vanquished enemies at home and abroad.

But what if there was a monument that took a different tack? Instead of celebrating power, it counseled against its abuses. Instead of celebrating the state and its works, it showed how these can become ruses to deceive and destroy. Instead of celebrating nationalist songs, symbols, and stories, it warned that these can be used as tools of division and oppression.

What if this museum was dedicated to memorializing one of history's most ghastly experiments in imperial conquest, demographic expulsion, and eventual extermination, to help us understand it and never repeat it?

Such a museum does exist. It is the US Holocaust Museum. It is the Beltway's most libertarian institution, a living rebuke to the worship of power as an end in itself.

I lived in Washington, D.C., when the Holocaust Museum was being built, and I vaguely recall when it opened. I never went, though I had the opportunity; I remember having a feeling of dread about the prospect of visiting it. Many people must feel the same way. Surely we already know that mass murder by the state is evil and wrong. Do we really need to visit a museum on such a ghastly subject?

The answer is *yes*. This institution is a mighty tribute to human rights and human dignity. It provides an intellectual experience more moving and profound than any I can recall having. It takes politics and ideas out of the realm of theory and firmly plants them in real life, in our own history. It shows the consequences of bad ideas in the hands of evil men, and invites you to experience the step-by-step descent into hell in chronological sThe transformation the visitor feels is intellectual but also even physical: as you approach the halfway point you notice an increase in your heart rate and even a pit in your stomach.

Misconceptions

Let's dispel a few myths that people who haven't visited might have about the place.

- The museum is not maudlin or manipulative. The narrative it takes you through is fact-based, focused on documentation (film and images), with a text that provides a careful chronology. One might even say it is a bit too dry, too merely factual. But the drama emerges from the contrast between the events and the calm narration.

- It is not solely focused on the Jewish victims; indeed, all victims of the National Socialism are discussed, such as the Catholics in Poland. But the history of Jewish persecution is also given great depth and perspective. It is mind boggling to consider how a regime that used anti-Semitism to manipulate the public and gain power ended up dominating most of Europe and conducting an extermination campaign designed to wipe out an entire people.

- The theme of the museum is not that the Holocaust was an inexplicable curse that mysteriously descended on one people at one time; rather the museum attempts to articulate and explain the actual reasons—the motives and ideology—behind the events, beginning with bad ideas that were only later realized in action when conditions made them possible.

- The narrative does not attempt to convince the visitor that the Holocaust was plotted from the beginning of Nazi rule; in fact, you discover a very different story. The visitor sees how bad ideas (demographic central planning; scapegoating of minorities; the demonization of others) festered, leading to ever worsening results: boycotts of Jewish-owned business, racial pogroms, legal restrictions on property and religion, internments, ghettoization, concentration camps, killings, and finally a carefully constructed and industrialized machinery of mass death.

- The museum does not isolate Germans as solely or uniformly guilty. Tribute is given to the German people, dissenters, and others who also fell victim to Hitler's regime. As for moral culpability, it unequivocally belongs to the Nazis and their compliant supporters in Germany and throughout Europe. But the free world also bears responsibility for shutting its borders to refugees, trapping Jews in a prison state and, eventually, execution chamber.

- The presentation is not rooted in sadness and despair; indeed, the museum tells of heroic efforts to save people from disaster and the resilience of the Jewish people in the face of annihilation. Even the existence of the museum is a tribute to hope because it conveys the conviction that we can learn from history and act in a way that never repeats this terrible past.

The Deeper Roots of the Holocaust

For the last two years, I've been steeped in studying and writing about the American experience with eugenics, the "policy science" of creating a master race. The more I've read, the more alarmed I've become that it was ever a thing, but it was all the rage in the Progressive Era. Eugenics was not a fringe movement; it was at the core of ruling-class politics, education, and culture. It was responsible for many of the early experiments in labor regulation. It was the driving force behind marriage licenses, minimum wages, restrictions on opportunities for women, and immigration quotas and controls.

The more I've looked into the subject, the more I'm convinced that it is not possible fully to understand the birth of the 20th century Leviathan without an awareness of eugenics. Eugenics was the original sin of the modern state that knows no limits to its power.

Once a regime decides that it must control human reproduction—to mold the population according to a central plan and divide human beings into those fit to thrive and those deserving extinction—you have the beginning of the end of freedom and civilization. The prophets of eugenics loathed the Jews, but also any peoples that they deemed dangerous to those they considered worthy of propagation. And the means they chose to realize their plans was top-down force.

So far in my reading on the subject, I've studied the origin of eugenics until the late 1920s, mostly in the US and the UK. And so, touring the Holocaust Museum was a revelation. It finally dawned on me: what happened in Germany was the extension and intensification of the same core ideas that were preached in the classrooms at Yale, Harvard, and Princeton decades earlier.

Eugenics didn't go away. It just took on a more violent and vicious form in different political hands. Without meaningful checks on state power, people with eugenic ambitions can find themselves lording over a terror state. It was never realized in the United States, but it happened elsewhere. The stuffy academic conferences of the 1910s, the mutton-chopped faces of the respected professorial class, mutated in one generation to become the camps and commandants of the Nazi killing machine. The distance between eugenics and genocide, from Boston to Buchenwald, is not so great.

There are moments in the tour when this connection is made explicit, as when it is explained how, prior to the Nazis, the United States had set the record for forced sterilizations; how Hitler cited the

US case for state planning of human reproduction; how the Nazis were obsessed with racial classification and used American texts on genetics and race as a starting point.

And think of this: when Progressive Era elites began to speak this way, to segment the population according to quality, and to urge policies to prevent "mongrelization," there was no "slippery slope" to which opponents could point. This whole approach to managing the social order was unprecedented, and so a historical trajectory was pure conjecture. They could not say "Remember! Remember where this leads!"

Now we have exactly that history, and a moral obligation to point to it and learn from it.

What Can We Learn?

My primary takeaway from knitting this history together and observing its horrifying outcome is this: that any ideology, movement, or demagogue that dismisses universal human rights, that disparages the dignity of any person based on group characteristics, that attempts to segment the population into the fit and unfit, or in any way seeks to use the power of the state to put down some in order to uplift others, is courting outcomes that are dangerous to the whole of humanity. It might not happen immediately, but, over time, such rhetoric can lay the foundations for the machinery of death.

And there is also another, perhaps more important lesson: bad ideas have a social and political momentum all their own, regardless of anyone's initial intentions. If you are not aware of that, you can be led down, step by step, to a very earthly hell.

At the same time, the reverse is also true: good ideas have a momentum that can lead to the flourishing of peace, prosperity, and universal human dignity. It is up to all of us. We must choose wisely, and never forget.

The Intellectual Conceit
of IQ Ideology

The cultural fascination with the idea of an "intelligence quotient" or IQ seems to be experiencing a resurgence. Relentless testing is a feature of schooling and school admissions, and tests are used for a variety of occupational screenings. The practice reflects an intuition we all have: some bulbs are brighter than others. Surely there is nothing wrong with knowing, measuring, and acting on that information, however difficult it might be to assess.

Where matters become elusive is in codifying those skills, reducing them all to a single quantitative number, aggregating them based on other demographic traits, assessing the variability of the results, comparing the results across large population groups, determining the variety of causal factors—genetic, environmental, sheer personal determination—that make up what we call intelligence, and cobbling together a plan for what to do with the results.

Here we have a much more complex problem, as complex as the human mind itself. The amateur commentator might read a book on the topic and hope to come away with a sense that within this literature we find the key to the rise and fall of whole civilizations. The would-be central planner salivates at the prospect! But the more you read, the less certain you become, and the more in awe of the unknowns, the surprises, and the way the real world continues to defy the predictions of the scientific elite.

The IQ as a Central Planning Tool

And then there are the social and political implications of the efforts. What's not usually understood is that the search for some measurable standard of intelligence—and implicitly human value itself—has a deep history that is bound up with the emergence of the planned society, eugenics, and the 20th century leviathan state.

That's hardly surprising. The notion of a scientific elite classifying people based on aptitude, assigning an efficient role for everyone, appeals to the conceit of intellectuals. While the curiosity about human biodiversity seems innocent, the birth of an ideology rooted in quantitative measurement of mental aptitude, backed by a scientistic planning ambition, obviously trends anti-liberal.

The story of IQ begins at the end of the Franco-Prussian war when France's civic institutions were remodeled to never lose another war. The prevailing theory was that France lacked the technical skills necessary for modern warfare. Citizens needed training and that meant education reform. Schooling would raise up a citizen army and therefore must be forced. From 1879 to 1886, legislation imposed compulsory schooling on the entire population.

With all kids now forced into non-religious schools, it was time to impose a rational method on steering the conscripts into socially and politically optimal paths. In 1904, just as fascination with the idea of scientific socialism had gained fashion, the French Ministry of Education contacted the psychologist Alfred Binet (1857–1911) to come up with some assessment test. He came up with a series of questions from easiest to hardest, and ranked the kids based on their performance of the tests.

The result was the Binet-Simon scale. From Binet's point of view, the only purpose was to identify which kids needed special focus and attention so that they would not be left behind. But the idea of quantity, ranking, and assessing cognitive performance caught on in the United States, whereeugenics was a prevailing intellectual fashion.

It was driving public policy in labor regulations, immigration, forced sterilizations, marriage licenses, welfare policy, business regulation, and segregation strategies.

The first American enthusiast for Binet's work was Henry H. Goddard, a leading champion of eugenics and a champion of the planning state. In 1908, Goddard translated Binet's work and popularized it among the intellectual classes. He turned what might have been a humanitarian push to provide remedial help to students into a weapon of war against the weak.

What did Goddard believe could be done with his insights?

He summarized his political outlook as follows:

> Democracy, then, means that the people rule by selecting the wisest, most intelligent, and most human to tell them what to do to be happy. Thus Democracy is a method for arriving at a truly benevolent aristocracy. Such a consummation will be reached when the most intelligent learn to apply their intelligence.... High intelligence must so work for the welfare of the masses as to command their respect and affection.

What's more, "society must be so organized that these people of limited intelligence shall not be given, or allowed to hold, positions that require more intelligence than they possess. And in the positions that they can fill, they must be treated in accordance with their level of intelligence. A society organized on this basis would be a perfect society."

Toward this end, he broke down the human population into normative categories, the underperforming of whom he labelled imbeciles, morons, and idiots—designations that survive to this day. He proposed a new form of social order in which an elite of intellectuals assigns tasks and life stations based on test results.

Illiberal at its Core

Yes, it sounds just like *Hunger Games*, *Divergent*, or any number of other dystopian nightmares because that is exactly what he imagined could be achieved with IQ studies. Having now read many dozens of books, articles, and contemporary accounts of this whole generation of thinkers, none of this comes as a surprise. Goddard's views were those of his generation, and they were the theorists of the totalitarian state— the "Progressives" in the United States, the post-Bismarckian planners of imperial Germany, the scientific socialists of Russia, and, later, the ghoulish exterminationists of Nazi Germany. It's all of a piece.

Continuing the tradition was Lewis Terman of Stanford who in 1916 proposed a revision to the now-traditional Binet test, and became an open and aggressive advocate of segregation, sterilization, immigration controls, birthing licenses, and a planned society generally.

White supremacy was a given among this generation, and he embraced it openly: "There is no possibility at present of convincing society that [Mexicans, Indians, and Negros] should not be allowed to reproduce, although from a eugenic point of view they constitute a grave problem because of their unusually prolific breeding." In that spirit, he joined the Human Betterment Foundation, which played the crucial role in California's sterilization program that had such a profound influence on the race policies of Hitler's Germany.

Intelligence tests became essential for a nation at war, with eugenicists advising the US Army about the fitness of soldiers: the dumbest at the front and the smartest in safe positions of leadership. And they advised immigration authorities: who could become an American and who couldn't. Eugenics was the goal and intelligence testing became a crucial part of the scientific veneer.

Thomas Leonard summarizes the bloody history:

> Dubious though the tests and testing methods were, the millions of persons subjected to crude intelligence tests demonstrated one result unambiguously.

American social scientists had convinced government
authorities to fund and compel human subjects for
an unprecedented measurement enterprise, carried
out to identify and cull inferiors, all in the name of
improving the efficiency of the nation's public schools,
immigration entry stations, institutions for the handi-
capped, and military.

That only begins to scratch the surface of the far-reaching hopes
of the IQ-eugenics movement. So close is the relationship between the
theory and policy ambition that they are really inseparable.

There seems to be nothing particularly threatening about wanting to assess an individual's aptitude. And yet IQ testing was created
and used as a social planning tool for use in compulsory education and
war preparation, and mutated into a full-scale ideology that had no
regard for human rights, the liberal theory of the social order, or freedom more generally. The eugenics movement, and its new tool of intelligence testing, hoped to replace freedom and dignity with totalitarian
technocracy.

What is it about this ideology that contradicts the idea of a free
society? Where is it that IQ ideology goes wrong?

There are three general issues:

**First, consumers have odd tastes that have little to do
with intelligence, scientifically defined.** Abstract Intelligence is
not necessarily the thing rewarded by the market, and that matters. In
a free society, the value of a resource is not objective; value is conferred
on services by the choices we make, whatever they may be.

If you hang out at NASCAR races, high intelligence is not the
first trait that stands out. Same with monster truck rallies. I might be
wrong of course. Maybe if I administered tests to all the participants
and consumers, I would be stunned at the disproportionate intelligence compared to the general population. The same goes for a Britney
Spears concert, an NFL game, or the buyers of grocery-store romance

novels. Maybe in these groups, you find higher intelligence than you find at the university chess club. I do seriously doubt it, however.

But the real question is: why does it matter? Does it matter whether Michael Phelps is smart or that he is the best swimmer in history? Swimming is what he valued for. It's the same way with Beyonce's singing and dancing or Matt Damon's acting. Or think of your favorite local restaurant: it actually doesn't matter whether the cook is smart or dumb.

The unpredictability of consumer markets defy intelligence distributions. Market processes are not about rewarding intelligence; they are about rewarding talent, insight, and service to others.

In fact, this is precisely why so many intellectuals have despised markets through the centuries. To them, it seems wrong that a professor of physics should make less than a pop star, that a number-crunching bureaucrat would live in a small house and a movie star own five mansions, and so on. Here is the source of more than a century of resentment against capitalism.

We all face resource constraints, time above all else. This is why we cooperate through trade with other people, even those with less absolute ability than we personally possess.

How markets value what they value will always remain unpredictable. What's crucial is that the common man is in charge of the system, and not planners. And that's the crux of the issue: who should decide what constitutes human value, who is worthy of being treated with dignity, who should be in charge of how labor resources are going to be used in society? Will we embrace freedom or rule by a wise elite?

Second, the law of association makes everyone valuable. A core belief of the IQ ideology is that smart people, as measured by tests, are more valuable to the social order than dumber people. But economics has made a different discovery. It turns out that through the division of labor, or what Ludwig von Mises called the "law of association," everyone can be valuable to everyone else, regardless of aptitude.

Michael Phelps might have the cognitive capacity to be the greatest nuclear physicist, computer programmer, or chess player in the world—but it is in his personal interest to focus on his comparative advantage, even if he has an absolute advantage over every person in the world.

We all face resource constraints, time above all else. This is why we cooperate through trade with other people, even those with less absolute ability than we personally possess. The result is more valuable than we could ever create on our own. You know this if you hire your lawn to be mowed, your house cleaned, or go to restaurants. Every social order consists of an infinitely complex web of relationships that defy categorization by crude scientific tests. Through the division of labor how freedom finds a way for everyone to become valuable to everyone else.

A third criticism of this literature is more profound. It observes that the intelligence necessary for the building of a great society does not reside in the minds of particular individuals. The highest intelligence of the social order resides in the processes and institutions of society itself. It doesn't exist in total in any single mind and it doesn't emerge consciously from the plans of any group.

Hayek explains in *The Counterrevolution of Science*:

> Though our civilization is the result of a cumulation of individual knowledge, it is not by the explicit or conscious combination of all this knowledge in any individual brain, but by its embodiment in symbols which we use without understanding them, in habits and institutions, tools and concepts, that man in society is constantly able to profit from a body of knowledge neither he nor any other man completely possesses. Many of the greatest things man has achieved are not the result of consciously directed thought, and still less the product of a deliberately co-ordinated effort of

many individuals, but of a process in which the individual plays a part which he can never fully understand. They are greater than any individual precisely because they result from the combination of knowledge more extensive than a single mind can master.

And there we see most plainly the difference between the IQ ideology and the theory of the free society. The IQ ideology tempts us to believe in the same fallacies that drove socialism: the conceit that a small elite, if given enough resources and power, can plan society better than the seemingly random associations, creations, and trades of individuals. Freedom, on the other hand, locates the brilliance of the social order not in the minds of a few, but in the process of social evolution itself and all the surprises and delights that entails.

The Eugenics Plot of the Minimum Wage

I n his "Letter from Birmingham Jail," Martin Luther King Jr. identi-
fies the government as the enemy of the rights and dignity of blacks.
He was locked up for marching without a permit. King cites the injus-
tices of the police and courts in particular. And he inspired a movement to raise public consciousness against state brutality, especially as
it involved fire hoses, billy clubs, and jail cells.

Less obvious, however, had been the role of a more covert means
of subjugation—forms of state coercion deeply embedded in the law
and history of the United States. And they were offered as policies
grounded in science and the scientific management of society.

Consider the minimum wage. How much does racism have to do
with it? Far more than most people realize. A careful look at its history shows that the minimum wage was originally conceived as part
of a eugenics strategy—an attempt to engineer a master race through
public policy designed to cleanse the citizenry of undesirables. To that
end, the state would have to bring about the isolation, sterilization, and
extermination of nonprivileged populations.

The eugenics movement—almost universally supported by the
scholarly and popular press in the first decades of the 20th century—
came about as a reaction to the dramatic demographic changes of
the latter part of the 19th century. Incomes rose and lifetimes had
expanded like never before in history. Such gains applied to all races

and classes. Infant mortality collapsed. All of this was due to a massive expansion of markets, technology, and trade, and it changed the world. It meant a dramatic expansion of population among all groups. The great unwashed masses were living longer and reproducing faster.

This trend worried the white ruling class in most European countries and in the United States. As John Carey documented in *Intellectuals and the Masses* (1992), all the founders of modern literary culture—from H.G. Wells to T.S. Elliot—loathed the new prosperity and variously spoke out on behalf of extermination and racial cleansing to put an end to newly emerging demographic trends. As Wells summed up, "The extravagant swarm of new births was the essential disaster of the nineteenth century."

The eugenics movement, as an application of the principle of the "planned society," was deeply hostile to free markets. As *The New Republic* summarized in a 1916 editorial:

> Imbecility breeds imbecility as certainly as white hens breed white chickens; and under laissez-faire imbecility is given full chance to breed, and does so in fact at a rate far superior to that of able stocks.

To counter the trends unleashed by capitalism, states and the national government began to implement policies designed to support "superior" races and classes and discourage procreation of the "inferior" ones. As explained by Edwin Black's 2003 book, *War Against the Weak: Eugenics and America's Campaign to Create a Master Race*, the goal as regards women and children was exclusionist, but as regards nonwhites, it was essentially exterminationist. The chosen means were not firing squads and gas chambers but the more peaceful and subtle methods of sterilization, exclusion from jobs, and coercive segregation.

It was during this period and for this reason that we saw the first trial runs of the minimum wage in Massachusetts in 1912. The new law pertained only to women and children as a measure to disemploy them and other "social dependents" from the labor force. Even though the measure was small and not well enforced, it did indeed reduce employment among the targeted groups.

To understand why this wasn't seen as a failure, take a look at the first modern discussions of the minimum wage appearing in the academic literature. Most of these writings would have been completely forgotten but for a seminal 2005 article in the *Journal of Economic Perspectives* by Thomas C. Leonard.

Leonard documents an alarming series of academic articles and books appearing between the 1890s and the 1920s that were remarkably explicit about a variety of legislative attempts to squeeze people out of the work force. These articles were not written by marginal figures or radicals but by the leaders of the profession, the authors of the great textbooks, and the opinion leaders who shaped public policy.

"Progressive economists, like their neoclassical critics," Leonard explains, "believed that binding minimum wages would cause job losses. However, the progressive economists also believed that the job loss induced by minimum wages was a social benefit, as it performed the eugenic service ridding the labor force of the 'unemployable.'"

At least the eugenicists, for all their pseudo-scientific blathering, were not naïve about the effects of wage floors. These days, you can count on media talking heads and countless politicians to proclaim how wonderful the minimum wage is for the poor. Wage floors will improve the standard of living, they say.

Back in 1912, they knew better—minimum wages exclude workers—and they favored them precisely *because* such wage floors drive people out of the job market. People without jobs cannot prosper and are thereby discouraged from reproducing. Minimum wages were designed specifically to purify the demographic landscape of racial inferiors and to keep women at the margins of society.

The famed Fabian socialist Sidney Webb was as blunt as anyone in his 1912 article "The Economic Theory of the Minimum Wage":

Legal Minimum Wage positively increases the productivity of the nation's industry, by ensuring that the surplus of unemployed workmen shall be exclusively the least efficient workmen; or, to put it in another way, by ensuring that all the situations shall be filled by the most efficient operatives who are available.

The intellectual history shows that whole purpose of the minimum wage was to *create* unemployment among people who the elites did not believe were worthy of holding jobs.

And it gets worse. Webb wrote:

What would be the result of a Legal Minimum Wage on the employer's persistent desire to use boy labor, girl labor, married women's labor, the labor of old men, of the feeble-minded, of the decrepit and broken-down invalids and all the other alternatives to the engagement of competent male adult workers at a full Standard Rate? ... To put it shortly, all such labor is parasitic on other classes of the community, and is at present employed in this way only because it is parasitic.

Further, Webb avers: "The unemployable, to put it bluntly, do not and cannot under any circumstances earn their keep. What we have to do with them is to see that as few as possible of them are produced."

Though Webb was writing about the experience in the United Kingdom, and his focus was on keeping the lower classes from flourishing, his views were not unusual. The same thinking was alive in the US context, but *race*, not class, became the decisive factor.

Henry Rogers Seager of Columbia University, and later president of the American Economic Association, laid it all out in "The Theory of the Minimum Wage" as published in the *American Labor Legislation Review* in 1913: "The operation of the minimum wage requirement would merely extend the definition of defectives to embrace all individuals, who even after having received special training, remain incapable of adequate self-support."

Further, he wrote, "If we are to maintain a race that is to be made of up of capable, efficient and independent individuals and family groups we must courageously cut off lines of heredity that have been proved to be undesirable by isolation or sterilization."

Isolation and sterilization of less desirable population groups are a form of slow-motion extermination. The minimum wage was part of that agenda. That was its purpose and intent. The opinion makers of 100 years ago were not shy about saying so. The policy was an important piece of weaponry in their eugenic war against nonelite population groups.

Princeton University's Royal Meeker was Woodrow Wilson's commissioner of labor. "It is much better to enact a minimum-wage law even if it deprives these unfortunates of work," Meeker argued in 1910. "Better that the state should support the inefficient wholly and prevent the multiplication of the breed than subsidize incompetence and unthrift, enabling them to bring forth more of their kind."

Frank Taussig, who was otherwise a good economist, asked in his bestselling textbook *Principles of Economics* (1911): "How to deal with the unemployable?"

They "should simply be stamped out," he stated.

> We have not reached the stage where we can proceed to chloroform them once and for all; but at least they can be segregated, shut up in refuges and asylums, and prevented from propagating their kind....
>
> What are the possibilities of employing at the prescribed wages all the healthy able-bodied who apply? The persons affected by such legislation would be those in the lowest economic and social group. The wages at which they can find employment depend on the prices at which their product will sell in the

market; or in the technical language of modern economics, on the marginal utility of their services. All
those whose additional product would so depress
prices that the minimum could no longer be paid by
employers would have to go without employment. It
might be practicable to prevent employers from paying any one less than the minimum; though the power
of law must be very strong indeed, and very rigidly
exercised, in order to prevent the making of bargains
which are welcome to both bargainers.

These are but a small sample and pertain only to this one policy.
Eugenics influenced other areas of American policy, too, especially
racial segregation. Obviously you can't have the races socializing and
partying together if the goal is to gradually exterminate one and boost
the population of the other. This goal was a driving force behind such
policies as regulations on dance clubs, for example. It was also a motivation behind the proliferation of marriage licenses, designed to keep the
unfit from marrying and reproducing.

But the minimum wage is in a special category because, these days,
its effects are so little understood. One hundred years ago, legislating
a price floor on wages was a policy deliberately conceived to impover-
ish the lower classes and the undesirables, and thereby to disincentivize
their reproduction. A polite gulag.

As time went on, the blood lust of the eugenics movement died
down, but the persistence of its minimum wage policies did not. A
national minimum wage passed in 1931 with the Davis-Bacon Act.
It required that firms receiving federal contracts pay prevailing wages,
which meant union wages, a principle that later became a national
minimum wage.

Speeches in support of the law were explicit about the fear that
black workers were undercutting the demands of white-only unions.
The minimum wage was a fix: it made it impossible to work for less.

The sordid history of the minimum wage law is harrowing in its intent but, at least, realistic about what wage floors actually do. *They stop upward mobility.*

Eugenics as an idea eventually lost favor after World War II, when it came to be associated with the Third Reich. But the labor policies to which it gave rise did not go away. They came to be promoted not as a method of exclusion and extermination but rather, however implausibly, as a positive effort to benefit the poor.

Whatever the intentions, the effects are still the same. On that the eugenicists were right. The eugenics movement, however evil its motive, understood an economic truth: the minimum wage excludes people from the job market. It takes away from marginal populations their most important power in the job market: the power to work for less. It cartelizes the labor market by allowing higher-wage groups access while excluding lower-wage groups.

King wrote of the cruelty of government in his day. That cruelty extends far back in time, and is crystallized by a wage policy that effectively makes productivity and upward mobility illegal. If we want to reject eugenic policies and the racial malice behind them, we should also repudiate the minimum wage and embrace the universal right to bargain.

The Misogynist Origins of American Labor Law

Many now credit government for past progress in gender equality, mostly because of late 20th-century legislation that appeared to benefit women in the workplace. This is a distorted view. Few know that government at all levels actually sought to prevent that progress.

A century ago, just as markets were attracting women to professional life, government regulation in the United States specifically targeted women to restrict their professional choices. The regulations were designed to drive them out of offices and factories and back into their homes—for their own good and the good of their families, their communities, and the future of the race.

The new controls—the first round of a century of interventions in the free labor market—were designed to curb the sweeping changes in economics and demographics that were taking place due to material advances in the last quarter of the 19th century. The regulations limited women's choices so they would stop making what elites considered the wrong decisions.

The real story, which is only beginning to emerge within the academic literature, is striking. It upends prevailing narratives about the relationship between government and women's rights. Many cornerstones of the early welfare and regulatory state were designed to hobble women's personal liberty and economic advancement. They were not progressive but reactionary, an attempt to turn back the clock.

Women's Work Is Not New

It was the freedom and opportunity realized in the latter period of the 19th century that changed everything for women workers, opening up new lines of employment.

The growth of industrial capitalism meant that women could leave the farm and move to the city. They could choose to leave home without having married—and even stay in the workforce as married women. They enjoyed more choice in education and professional life than ever before.

By 1910, fully 45 percent of the professional workforce was made up of women. They almost entirely dominated the teaching profession, for example. Single women increasingly found work as nurses, librarians, secretaries, and social workers, as well as factory workers in the garment industry. Women, most of them unmarried, constituted 21 percent of the entire workforce.

New clerical jobs, unknown a century earlier, were everywhere to be had. Women's wages were rising quickly, by an impressive 16 percent from 1890 through 1920. Nor were women working at "exploitative" wages. A Rand corporation study of wage differentials discovered an interesting fact: women's wages relative to men's were higher in 1920 than they were in 1980.

The Law Intervenes

And yet, these were also the years in which we first saw government intervention in the labor market, much of it specifically targeting women. As historian Thomas Leonard argues in his spectacular book *Illiberal Reformers* (2016), an entire generation of intellectuals and politicians panicked about what this could mean for the future of humanity.

Society must control reproduction and therefore what women do with their lives. So said the prevailing ideology of the age. We couldn't have a situation in which markets enticed women to leave the control of their families and move to the city.

Though they are called Progressives, the reformers' rhetoric had more in common with the "family values" movement of the 1970s and '80s—with pseudoscientific race paranoia playing the role that religion would later play. In many ways, they were the ultimate conservatives, attempting to roll back the tide of history made possible by the advance of the capitalist economy.

They were incredibly successful. Over a 10-year period between 1909 and 1919, 40 states restricted the number of hours that women employees could work. Fifteen states passed new minimum wage laws to limit entry-level jobs. Most states created stipends for single-parent families, specifically to incentivize women to reject commercial life, return to protected domesticity, and stop competing with men for wages.

Such laws were completely new in American history (and in almost all of modern history) because they intervened so fundamentally in the right of workers and employers to make any sort of contract. The Progressive agenda involved government deeply in issues that directly affected people's ability to provide for themselves. It also created unprecedented impositions on both employees and their employers. Such laws would have been inconceivable even 50 years earlier.

How did all this happen so fast, and why?

The Inferiority of Women

Richard T. Ely, the hugely influential founder of the American Economic Association and the godfather of progressive economics, explained the issue clearly, laying the groundwork for the laws that followed. His 1894 book *Socialism and Social Reform* expressed a panic about women's entry into the workforce.

> Restrictions should be thrown about the employ-
> ment of married women, and their employment for

a considerable period before and after child-birth
should be prohibited under any circumstances. There
should also be a restriction of the work-day, as in England, for children and young persons under eighteen,
and for women. Such a limitation having beneficial
effect upon the health of the community.... Night
work should be prohibited for women and persons
under eighteen years of age and, in particular, all work
injurious to the female organism should be forbidden
to women.

If the reference to the "female organism" sounds strange, remember that this generation of intellectuals believed in eugenics—using
state force to plan the emergence of the model race—and hence saw
women mainly as propagators of the race, not human individuals with
the right to choose. For anyone who believed that government had a
responsibility to plan human production (and most intellectuals at the
time did believe this), the role of women was critical. They couldn't be
allowed to do what they wanted, go where they wanted, or make lives
for themselves. This was the normal thought pattern for the generation that gave the United States unprecedented legal restrictions on the
labor market.

The Supreme Court Weighs In

Consider the Supreme Court case of *Muller v. Oregon*, which considered state legislation on maximum working hours and decided in
favor of the state. Oregon was hardly unusual; it was typical of the 20
states that had already passed such laws directed at women's freedom to
choose employment. From the text of Colorado's law passed in 1903:
"No woman" shall "work or labor for a greater number than eight hours
in the twenty-four hour day ... where such labor, work, or occupation by
its nature, requires the woman to stand or be upon her feet."

The decision in *Muller v. Oregon*, then, ratified such laws all over the country. Today, this case is widely considered the foundation of progressive labor law. What's not well known is that the brief that settled the case was a remarkable piece of pseudoscience that argued for the inferiority of women and hence their need for special protections from the demands of commercial enterprise. That brief was filed by future Supreme Court justice Louis Brandeis.

The Weird and Awful "Brandeis Brief"

The "Brandeis Brief" argued that the law had to stop the massive influx of women into the workplace because women have "special susceptibility to fatigue and disease," because female blood has more water in it than men's blood. Their blood composition also accounts for why women have less focus, energy, and strength generally, according to the brief.

"Physicians are agreed that women are fundamentally weaker than men in all that makes for endurance: in muscular strength, in nervous energy, in the powers of persistent attention and application."

Moreover, "In strength as well as in rapidity and precision of movement women are inferior to men. This is not a conclusion that has ever been contested."

Long hours are "more disastrous to the health of women than to men," the brief explained. Government therefore needed to regulate work hours for the "health, safety, morals, and general welfare of women."

Restrictions on work hours were therefore essential. "It is of great hygienic importance on account of the more delicate physical organization of woman," the brief said, "and will contribute much toward the better care of children and the maintenance of a regular family life."

This brief is also notable for being the first to combine science, however bogus, and public policy in an appeal to the Supreme Court.

Florence Kelley's Dream of Nonworking Women

One might suspect that the entire effort was a male-driven one to stop female progress, but that's not the case. A leader in the campaign for such labor interventions was writer and activist Florence Kelley. Modern progressives celebrate her activism for maximum work hours, the 10-hour workday, minimum wages, and children's rights. Indeed, she is considered a great hero by the sanitized version of history that progressives tell each other.

Before we cheer her accomplishments, however, we should look at Kelley's driving motivation. Writing in the *American Journal of Sociology*, she explained that she wanted a minimum wage as a wage floor to stop manufacturing plants and retail outlets from employing women for less than they could otherwise employ men.

Retail stores, she wrote, tend to "minimize the employment of men, substituting them for women, girls, and boys, employed largely at less than living wages." It was precisely such competition from women and children that Kelley intended to stop, so that men could earn higher wages and women could return to traditional roles.

In her book *Some Ethical Gains through Legislation* (1905), Kelley said that long working hours had to be ended for women because commercial life was introducing "vice" into communities ("vice" for this generation was the preferred euphemism for every manner of sexual sin). Worse, women were choosing commercial life over home "on their own initiative."

Kelley considered it necessary to restrict women's rights for their own "health and morality," she said, and also to boost men's wages so women would stay home under the care of their mothers, fathers, suitors, and husbands.

Moreover, to make such work illegal would make "righteous living" more practical for women. If they stopped being rewarded in wages, they would return to domestic life. Kelley even regretted the invention of electricity because it allowed women to work late at factories, when they should be at home reading to children by firelight.

In Kelley's view, the ideal role of women with children is not to enter commercial life at all: "Family life in the home is sapped in its foundation when mothers of young children work for wages." It's an opinion with which some may still sympathize, but should such an opinion be imposed on working families by coercive legislation? For this paragon of progressive social reform, it was clear that lawmakers had to force women back into the home.

Florence Kelley and the movement she represented sought to disemploy women and get everyone back to a premodern form of domestic living. She wanted not more rights for women but fewer. The workplace was properly for men, who were to get paid high wages sufficient for the whole family. That was the basis for her support of a range of legislation to drive women out of the workforce and put an end to the new range of options available to them, options that many women were happy to choose.

Fear the Women of East Prussia

All this scholarship and activism is one thing, but what about the popular press?

Professor Edward A. Ross, author of *Sin and Society*, spoke out in the *New York Times* on May 3, 1908. In an article titled "The Price Woman Pays to Industrial Progress," Ross warned that America's "fine feminine form" was endangered by commercial society.

If women were permitted to work, an evolutionary selection process would govern their reproduction to the detriment of the human race. The graceful women who would otherwise bear beautiful children would be pushed out of the gene pool and replaced by "squat, splay-footed, wide-backed, flat-breasted, broad-faced, short-necked—a type that lacks every grace that we associate with women."

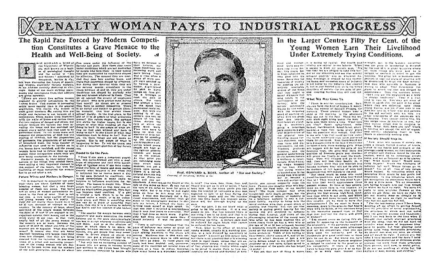

Ross's example: "the women of East Prussia," who "bear a child in the morning" and "are out in the field in the afternoon."

The professor explained that women who had worked in factories would not make suitable bearers of children. "Think of the discouraging situation of the young man who after he has been married two or three years finds he has a wife who at the age of 28 or 30 has collapsed, become a miserable invalid, suffering aches and pains all the time." Why, she might find herself "unable to keep the home attractive." And all of this "because of just a few extra dollars added to the profits of the employer or a few extra dollars saved to the consumer."

Because of the dangerous combination of employment and natural selection, Ross contended, the government had to extend a hand to help these women by limiting working hours and establishing a high bar to enter the workforce: minimum wages.

Only through such enlightened interventions could government save women from the workplace, so that they could return to the maternal duties of rearing "girls who have the qualities of fineness— grace and charm."

Is This Satire?

If this reads like satire, sadly it is not. Nor were such views unusual in a generation of ruling-class intellectuals, politicians, and activists that embraced eugenics and rejected capitalism as too random, too chaotic, too liberating. Their plan was to reestablish and entrench by law the family and marital structure they believed in, which absolutely precluded a generation of women making individual choices over their own lives.

Every trend panicked the eugenic generation. They fretted about the falling birth rate among those who should be reproducing and the rising birth rate among those who shouldn't be. They worried about morals, about competition, about health, about culture. Most of all, they regretted the change that a dynamic economy was bringing about.

Thus, from 1900 through 1920, a period that set the stage for a century of interventions in the labor market, hundreds of laws stifling women were passed in every state and at the federal level, too. None dared call it misogyny, but this is real history, however rarely it is told.

Feminists against Regulation

Laws that disemployed thousands of women nationwide led to vast protests. The Equal Opportunity League, an early feminist organization in New York, lobbied the state legislature to repeal the bans on work. And it received quite the press coverage.

"So-called 'welfare' legislation is not asked for or wanted by real working women," the league said. "These 'welfare' bills are drafted by self-styled social uplifters who assert that working women do not know enough to protect themselves."

"Are women people? Women are no longer the wards of the State and a law that is unconstitutional for a man voter is equally unconstitutional for a woman voter."

"Working at night is not more injurious than working in the

WOMEN'S WORK LIMITED BY LAW

Equal Opportunity League Fighting Legislation Which Restricts Their Hours of Labor

WOMEN actively interested in labor conditions affecting women workers, especially with reference to legislation considered as discriminating against women under a disguise of beneficial purpose, have begun a determined fight to prevent the passage by the New York State Legislature of three new labor measures and for the repeal of two laws limiting hours of employment.

Petitions are being sent to members of the Assembly and the State Senate pleading that women be protected in their right to equal opportunity with men in the industrial fields. The Women's Equal Opportunity League, representing more than 20,000 women, is actively engaged in the campaign. In the appeals to the Legislature the league complains of cases of severe financial loss, deprivation of the right to choose the most favorable hours of employment, and, in some cases, the compulsory abandonment of profitable

women in factories to eight hours a day (forty-eight hours a week), prohibiting even five minutes of overtime and work on a night shift after 9 P. M. or before 6 A. M.

As an indication of the injustice that would be done to women should this bill become law are cited the effects of a similar though less drastic law which is now in force. The fifty-four-hour-week-and-no-night-work law now applying to factories has resulted in the elimination of highly skilled woman labor from the better-paying trades and professions having a basic eight-hour day, for the simple reason that it was against the law to have women work overtime in rush seasons or to transfer them to a night shift if and when desirable (although the night shift is usually less than eight hours and the wage is higher). If the pending bill becomes a law women will be ousted from all classes of work where the wage is high enough to attract men, and they will be forced back into the canneries, textile mills,

can be shifted from day to night work as occasion may demand.

With regard to the requirement of this law that seats be installed in all elevators (or lifts) operated by women, it is said that it is extremely dangerous to operate an elevator while sitting, and for this reason all elevator operators, both men and women, are given occasional rest periods in the course of the day. "Therefore, the provision requiring with such tender concern that women operators shall be seated while running an elevator is obviously intended to further disqualify them for work."

In short, the conclusion of the league is "that these proposed bills and laws, ostensibly intended to protect and shield the woman worker, will, if permitted to stand, unquestionably work her industrial ruin and throw her back into the slough of drudgery out of which she is just emerging after centuries of painful, laborious effort to better her condition."

"If women," the Equal Opportunity

daytime," the league argued. "Many women prefer to work at night because the wage is higher, opportunities for advancement greater, and women with children can enjoy being with their child after school hours in the day time."

In fact, the phrase "equal pay for equal work" was not created to mandate higher wages for women. It was a league slogan invoked to argue against laws that made it "a crime to employ women even five minutes after the eight-hour day." The phrase emerged as a preferred slogan to protest *in favor of free markets*, not against them.

The Equal Opportunity League also passionately opposed the minimum wage law. Such laws, it argued, "while purporting to be for [women's] benefit, would really be a serious handicap to them in competing with men workers for desirable positions."

In short, the conclusion of the League is that these proposed bills and laws, ostensibly intended to protect and shield the woman worker, will, if permitted to stand, unquestionably work her industrial ruin and throw her back into the slough of drudgery out of which she is just emerging after centuries of painful, laborious effort to better her condition. ("Women's Work Limited by Law," *New York Times*, January 18, 1920)

Restriction Becomes Liberation?

The fairy tale version of history says that during the 20th century, government freed women to become newly empowered in the workplace. The reality is exactly the opposite. Just as the market was granting women more choices, government swept in to limit them in the name of health, purity, family values, and social uplift. Such laws and regulations are still around today, though they have been recharacterized in a completely different way. As Orwell might say, somewhere along the way, restriction became liberation.

IV
THE PHILOSOPHY

Five Differences Between the Alt-Right and Libertarianism

Well, Hillary Clinton has gone and done it.

To the cheers of alt-righters everywhere, those angry lords of the green frog meme who hurl edgy un-PC insults at everyone to their left, the Democratic nominee has put them on the map at long last. Specifically, she accused Donald Trump of encouraging and giving voice to their dark and dangerous worldview.

Let's leave aside the question of whether we are talking about an emergent brown-shirted takeover of American political culture, or perhaps merely a few thousand sock-puppet social media accounts adept at mischievous trolling on Twitter. The key issue is that more than a few alt-rightists claim some relationship to libertarianism, at least at their intellectual dawning until they begin to shed their libertarianism later on.

What are the differences in outlook between alt-right ideology and libertarianism?

1. The Driving Force of History

Every ideology has a theory of history, some sense of a driving theme that causes episodic movements from one stage to another. Such a theory helps us make sense of the past, present, and future. The libertarian theme of history is beautifully articulated by Murray Rothbard:

My own basic perspective on the history of man...is to place central importance on the great conflict which is eternally waged between Liberty and Power... I see the liberty of the individual not only as a great moral good in itself (or, with Lord Acton, as the highest political good), but also as the necessary condition for the flowering of all the other goods that mankind cherishes: moral virtue, civilization, the arts and sciences, economic prosperity. Out of liberty, then, stem the glories of civilized life.

There it is: liberty vs. power. Liberty unleashes human energy and builds civilization. Anything that interferes with the progress of liberty impedes the progress of humanity. One crowds out the other. The political (or anti-political) goal is clear: diminish power (which means reducing unjust violence) and enhance liberty.

What is the alt-right theory of history? The movement inherits a long and dreary tradition of thought from Friedrich Hegel to Thomas Carlyle to Oswald Spengler to Madison Grant to Othmar Spann to Giovanni Gentile to Carl Schmitt to Trump's speeches. This tradition sees something else going on in history: not liberty vs. power, but something like a more meta struggle that concerns impersonal collectives of tribe, race, community, great men, and so on.

Whereas libertarianism speaks of individual choice, alt-right theory draws attention to collectives on the move. It imagines that despite appearances, we all default in our thinking back to some more fundamental instinct about our identity as a people, which is either being shored up by a more intense consciousness or eroded by a deracination and dispossession from what defines us. To criticize this as racist is often true but superficial. What's really going on here is the depersonalization of history itself: the principle that we are all being buffeted about by Olympian historical forces beyond our control as mere individuals. Each of us only matters when our uniqueness is submerged to a group. This group in turn calls forth a leader. It takes something mighty and ominous like a great leader, an embodiment of one of these great forces, to make a dent in history's narrative.

2. Harmony vs. Conflict

A related issue concerns our capacity to get along with each other. Frédéric Bastiat described the free society as characterized by a "harmony of interests." In order to overcome the state of nature, we gradually discover the capacity to find value in each other. The division of labor is the great fact of human community: the labor of each of us becomes more productive in cooperation with others, and this is even, or rather especially, true given the unequal distribution of talents, intelligence, and skills, and differences over religion, belief systems, race, language, and so on.

And truly, this is a beautiful thing to discover. The libertarian marvels at the cooperation we see in a construction project, an office building, a restaurant, a factory, a shopping mall, to say nothing of a city, a country, or a planet. The harmony of interests doesn't mean that everyone gets along perfectly, but rather that we inhabit institutions that incentivize progress through ever more cooperative behavior. As the liberals of old say, we believe that the "brotherhood of man" is possible.

To the alt-right mind, this all seems ridiculous. Sure, shopping is fine. But what actually characterizes human association is deep-rooted conflict. The races are secretly at war, intellectually and genetically. There is an ongoing and perpetual conflict between the sexes. People of different religions must fight and always will, until one wins. Nations fight for a reason: the struggle is real.

Some argue that war is what defines us and even gives life meaning, and, in that sense, is glorious and celebratory. For this reason, all nations must aspire toward homogeneity in stock, religion, and so on, and, as for the sexes, there must be dominance, because cooperation is an illusion.

Maybe you notice a certain commonality with the left here. In the 19th century, the Marxists whipped themselves up in a frenzy about the allegedly inherent conflict between labor and capital. Their successors fret incessantly about race, ethnicity, ability, gender, and so on, pushing Marxian conflict theory into ever more exotic realms. Ludwig von Mises captured this parallel brilliantly when he wrote, "Nationalist ideology divides society vertically; the socialist ideology divides society horizontally." Here, as with many other areas, the far right and far left are strangely aligned.

3. Designed vs. Spontaneous Order

The libertarian believes that the best and most wonderful social outcomes are not those planned, structured, and anticipated, but rather the opposite. Society is the result of millions and billions of small acts of rational self interest that are channeled into an undesigned, unplanned, and unanticipated order that cannot be conceived by a single mind. The knowledge that is required to put together a functioning social order is conveyed through institutions: prices, manners, mores, habits, and traditions that no one can consciously will into existence. There must be a process in place, and stable rules governing that process, that permit such institutions to evolve, always in deference to the immutable laws of economics.

Again, the alt-right mind finds all of this uninspired and uninspiring. Society in their conception is built by the will of great thinkers and great leaders with unconstrained visions of what can be. What we see out there operating in society is a result of someone's intentional and conscious planning from the top down.

If we cannot find the source, or if the source is somehow hiding, we imagine that it must be some shadowy group out there that is manipulating outcomes—and hence the alt-right's obsession with conspiracy theory. The course of history is designed by someone, so "we" might as well engage in the great struggle to seize the controls—and hence the alt-right obsession with politics as a contact sport.

Oh, and, by the way, economics is a dismal science because, according to Thomas Carlyle, it opposes

4. Trade and Migration

Of course the classical liberals fought for free trade and free migration of peoples, seeing national borders as arbitrary lines on a map that mercifully restrain the power of the state but otherwise inhibit the progress of prosperity and civilization. To think globally is not a bad thing, but a sign of enlightenment. Protectionism is nothing but a tax on consumers that inhibits industrial productivity and sets nations at odds with each other. The market process is a worldwide phenomenon that indicates an expansion of the division of labor, which means a progressive capacity of people to enhance their standard of living and ennoble their lives.

The alt-right is universally opposed to free trade and free migration. You can always tell a writer is dabbling in alt-right thought (or neoreactionary or Dark Enlightenment or outright fascism) if he or she has an intense focus on international trade as inherently bad or fraudulent or regrettable in some sense. To them, a nation must be strong enough to thrive as an independent unit, an economic sovereignty unto itself.

Today, the alt-right has a particular beef with trade deals, not because they are unnecessarily complex or bureaucratic (which are good reasons to doubt their merit) but because of their meritorious capacity to facilitate international cooperation. And it is the same with immigration. Beginning at some point in the late 19th century, migration came to be seen as a profound threat to national identity, which invariably means racial identity.

5. Emancipation and Progress

The libertarian celebrates the profound changes in the world from the late Middle Ages to the age of laissez faire, because we observed how commercial society broke down the barriers of class, race, and social isolation, bringing rights and dignity to ever more people. Slavery was ended. Women were emancipated, as marriage evolved from conquest and dominance into a free relationship of partnership and consent. This is all a wonderful thing, because rights are universal, which is to say, they rightly belong to everyone equally. Anything that interferes with people's choices holds them back and hobbles the progress of prosperity, peace, and human flourishing. This perspective necessarily makes the libertarian optimistic about humanity's potential.

The alt-right mind can't bear this point of view, and regards it all as naive. What appears to be progress is actually loss: loss of culture, identity, and mission. They look back to what they imagine to be a golden age when elites ruled and peons obeyed. And thus we see the source of their romantic attachment to authority as the source of order, and the longing for authoritarian political rule. As for universal rights, forget it. Rights are granted by political communities and are completely contingent on culture. The ancients universally believed that some were born to serve and some to rule, and the alt-right embraces this perspective. Here again, identity is everything and the loss of identity is the greatest crime against self anyone can imagine.

Conclusion

To be sure, as many commentators have pointed out, both libertarians and alt-rightist are deeply suspicious of democracy. This was not always the case. In the 19th century, the classical liberals generally had a favorable view of democracy, believing it to be the political analogy to choice in the marketplace. But here they imagined states that were local, rules that were fixed and clear, and democracy as a check on power. As states became huge, as power became total, and as rules became subject to pressure-group politics, the libertarian attitude toward democracy shifted.

In contrast, the alt-right's opposition to democracy traces to its loathing of the masses generally and its overarching suspicion of anything that smacks of equality. In other words, they tend to hate democracy for all the wrong reasons. This similarity is historically contingent and largely superficial given the vast differences that separate the two worldviews. Does society contain within itself the capacity for self management or not? That is the question.

None of this will stop the mainstream media from lumping us all together, given that we share a dread of what has become of the left in politics today.

But make no mistake: the alt-right knows exactly who its enemies are, and the libertarians are among them.

The Prehistory of
the Alt-right

Reading "Why I Left the Left" is a solid reminder that there's not much intellectual heft remaining on that side of the fence. If an ideology sets out to isolate the locus of evil in people's very identity, it is pretty well spent. This, in addition to the failure of the socialist model everywhere it has tried, explains why the Left has suffered so much at the polls and now faces a serious backlash in campus and public life.

With the failure of action comes reaction, and now the Western world is dealing with something far less familiar to most people: the rise of the alt-right as the alternative. It is attractive to some young people due to its taboo-breaking, rebel ethos that so easily inflames teachers and protectors of civic conventions.

The movement is more than that, however. It has a real philosophical and political history, one that stands in violent opposition to the idea of individual liberty. It has been largely suppressed since World War II and, because of that, most people assumed fascism (and its offshoots) was gone from the earth.

As a result, this generation has not been philosophically prepared to recognize the tradition, the signs, the implications, and the political application of the ideology so many are stumbling to embrace.

Here is a prehistory of what we call the alt-right today, which is probably better described as a 21st-century incarnation of what in the 19th century would have been called right-Hegelianism. I'm skipping over many political movements (in Spain, France, and Italy), and clownish leaders like George Lincoln Rockwell, Oswald Mosley, and Fr. Coughlin, to get right to the core ideas that form something like a school of thought which developed over a century.

Here we have a lineage of non-Marxist, non-leftist brand of right-ist but still totalitarian thinking, developed in fanatical opposition to bourgeois freedom.

1820: Georg Friedrich Hegel published *Elements of the Philosophy of Right*, which spelled out the political implications of his "dialectical idealism," an outlook that departed dramatically from the liberal tradition by completely abstracting from human experience to posit warring life forces operating beyond anyone's control to shape history. It turns out that the politics of this view amounted to "the state is the march of God through the world." He looked forward to some age in the future that would realize the apotheosis of State control. The Hegelian view, according to a 1952 lecture by Ludwig von Mises, broke into Left and Right branches, depending on the attitude toward nationalism and religion (the right supported the Prussian state and church, whereas the left did not), and thereby "destroyed German thinking and German philosophy for more than a century, at least."

1841: Thomas Carlyle published *On Heroes, Hero-Worship, and The Heroic in History*, which popularized the "great man" theory of history. History is not about marginal improvements in living standards by using better tools, but rather about huge episodic shifts brought about through power. A champion of slavery and opponent of liberalism, Carlyle took aim at the rise of commercial society, praising Cromwell, Napoleon, and Rousseau, and rhapsodizing about the glories of power. "The Commander over Men; he to whose will our wills are to be subordinated, and loyally surrender themselves, and find their welfare in doing so, may be reckoned the most important of Great Men." Carlyle's target was Adam Smith and the Scottish Enlightenment generally. Hitler's biographers agree that the words of Carlyle were the last he requested to be read to him before he died.

1841: On the continent, meanwhile, Friedrich List published *The National System of Political Economy*, celebrating protectionism, infrastructure spending, and government control and support of industry. Again, it was a direct attack on laissez faire and a celebration of the national unit as the only truly productive force in economic life. Steven Daviescomments: "The most serious result of List's ideas was a change in people's thinking and perception. Instead of seeing trade as a cooperative process of mutual benefit, politicians and businessmen came to regard it as a struggle with winners and losers." Today's economic nationalists have nothing new to add to the edifice already constructive by List.

1871: Charles Darwin left the realm of science briefly to enter sociological analysis with his book *The Descent of Man*. It is a fascinating work but tended to treat human society as a zoological rather than sociological and economic enterprise. It included an explosive paragraph (qualified and widely misread) that regretted how "we institute poor-laws; and our medical men exert their utmost skill to save the life of every one to the last moment... Thus the weak members of civilized societies propagate their kind. No one who has attended to the breeding of domestic animals will doubt that this must be highly injurious to the race of man." At the very least, he suggested, we should stop the weak from marrying. This is the "one check" we have to keep society from being taken over by inferiors. Tragically, this passing comment-fired up the eugenicists who immediately began to plot demographic planning schemes to avoid a terrifying biological slide to universal human degeneracy.

1896: The American Economic Association published *Race Traits and Tendencies of the American Negro* by Frederick Hoffman. This monograph, one of many of the type, described blacks as intractable criminals who are both lazy and promiscuous, the influence of whom in national biology can only lead to a decline of the race. Their mere presence was considered an existential threat to "uncompromising virtues of the Aryan race." Such views were embraced by Richard T. Ely, the founder of the American Economic Association, and came to dominate the academic journals of this period, providing academic cover for Jim Crow laws, state segregation, business regulation, and far worse.

1904: The founder of the American eugenics society, Charles Davenport, established the Station for Experimental Evolution and worked to propagate eugenics from his perch as Professor of Zoology at Harvard University. He was hugely influential on an entire generation of scientists, political figures, economists, and public bureaucrats, and it was due largely to this influence that eugenics became such a central concern of American policies from this period until World War II, influencing the passage of wage legislation, immigration, marriage licenses, working hours legislation, and, of course, mandatory sterilizations

At this point in history, all five pillars of fascist theory (historicist, nationalist, racist, protectionist, statist) were in place. It had a theory of history. It had a picture of hell, which is liberalism and uncontrolled commercial society. It had a picture of heaven, which was national societies run by great men inhabiting all-powerful States focused on heavy industry. It had a scientific rationale.

Above all, it had an agenda: to control society from the top down with the aim of managing every aspect of the demographic path of human society, which meant controlling human beings from cradle to grave to produce the most superior product, as well as industrial planning to replace the wiles of the market process. The idea of freedom itself, to this emergent school of thought, was a disaster for everyone everywhere.

All that was really necessary was popularization of its most incendiary ideas.

1916: Madison Grant, scholar of enormous prestige and elite connections,published *The Passing of the Great Race*. It was never a bestseller but it exercised enormous influence among the ruling elites, and made a famous appearance in F. Scott Fitzgerald's *The Great Gatsby*. Grant, an early environmentalist, recommended mass sterilization of people as a "practical, merciful, and inevitable solution of the whole problem" that should be "applied to an ever-widening circle of social discards, beginning always with the criminal, the diseased, and the insane, and extending gradually to types which may be called weaklings rather than defectives, and perhaps ultimately to worthless race types." Hitler loved the book and sent Grant a note praising the book as his personal bible.

1919: Following World War I, German historian Oswald Spengler published *The Decline of the West*, which met with huge popular acclaim for capturing the sense of the moment: the cash economy and liberalism were dead and could only be replaced by the rise of monolithic cultural forms that rally around blood and race as the source of meaning. Blood beats money all over the world, he argued. The interminable and foggy text broods with right-Hegelian speculations about the status of man and predicts the complete downfall of all lovely things unless the civilization of the West dispenses with its attachment to commercial norms and individualism and instead rallies to the cause of group identity. The book kicked off a decade of similar works and movements that declared freedom and democracy to be dead ideas: the only relevant battle was between the communist and fascist forms of state planning.

1932: Carl Schmitt published *The Concept of the Political*, a brutal attack on liberalism as the negation of the political. For Schmitt, the political was the essence of life, and the friend/enemy distinction is its most salient feature. Friends and enemies were to be defined by the State, and enemy-ness can only be fully instantiated in bloodshed, which should be real and present. Mises called him "the Nazi Jurist" for a reason: he was a party member and his ideas contributed mightily to the perception that mass death was not only moral, but essential to the preservation of the meaning of life itself.

1944: Allied troops discovered thousands of death camps strewn throughout Nazi-captured territories in Europe, created beginning in 1933 and continuing through the duration of the war, responsible for the imprisonment and death of upwards of 15 million people. The discovery shocked an entire generation at the most fundamental level, and the scramble was on to discover all sources of evil—political and ideological—that had led to such a gruesome reality. With the Nazi forces defeated and the Nuremberg trials underscoring the point, the advance of fascist dogma in all of its brooding, racist, statist, and historicist timbres, came to a screeching halt. Suppression of the ideas therein began in Europe, the United Kingdom, and the United States, creating the impression that right-Hegelianism was a mere flash in the pan that had been permanently doused by state power.

The same year as the death-camp discovery began, F.A. Hayek published *The Road to Serfdom*, which emphasized that it was not enough to reject the labels, songs, slogans, and regimes of Nazism and fascism. Also necessary, said Hayek, was the rejection of the ideas of planning themselves, which even in a democracy necessarily led to the end of freedom and the rise of dictatorship. His book was met with critical acclaim among a small group of remaining classical liberals (many of whom were involved in the founding of FEE two years later) but was otherwise denounced and derided as paranoid and reactionary by many others.

For the duration of the ensuing Cold War, it was the fear of communism and not fascism/Nazism that would captivate the public mind. After all, the latter had been defeated on the battlefield, right? The genesis and development of rightest totalitarianism, despite the earnest pleadings of Hannah Arendt, fell away from public consciousness.

Liberalism Not Yet

The Cold War ended 25 years ago and the rise of digital technology has given liberal forms of political economy a gigantic presence in the world. Trade has never been more integrated. Human rights are on the march. Commercial life, and its underlying ideology of harmony and peace, is the prevailing aspiration of billions of people around the world. The failures of government planning are ever more obvious. And yet these trends alone do not seal the deal for the cause of liberty.

With left-Hegelianism now in disgrace, political movements around the world are rooting around in the pre-war history of totalitarian ideas to find alternatives. The suppression of these ideas did not work; in fact, they had the opposite effect of making them more popular to the point where they boiled up from below. The result is what we call the Alt-right in the US and goes by many other names in Europe and the UK. (The transition from the 1990s to the present will be the subject of another essay.)

Let us not be deceived. Whatever the flavor—whichever branch of Hegel we choose to follow—the cost of government control is human liberty, prosperity, and dignity. We choose mega-states, strongmen, national planning, or religious and racial homogeneity at our deep peril.

For the most part, the meme-posting trolls who favor stormfront-style profile pics on their social accounts, and the mass movements calling for strongmen to take control and cast the other from their midst, are clueless about the history and path they are following.

If you are feeling tempted toward the Alt-right, look at your progenitors: do you like what you see?

What is the alternative to right and left Hegelianism? It is found in the liberal tradition, summed up by Frederic Bastiat's phrase "the harmony of interests." Peace, prosperity, liberty, and community are possible. It is this tradition, and not one that posits intractable war between groups, that protects and expands human rights and human dignity, and creates the conditions that allow for the universal ennoblement of the human person.

The last word on the correct (freedom-loving) path forward was framed by the great English historian Thomas Babington Macaulay in 1830, a statement that would be loathed by every fascist in history:

> It is not by the intermeddling of an omniscient and omnipotent State, but by the prudence and energy of the people, that England has hitherto been carried forward in civilization; and it is to the same prudence and the same energy that we now look with comfort and good hope. Our rulers will best promote the improvement of the nation by strictly confining themselves to their own legitimate duties, by leaving capital to find its most lucrative course, commodities their fair price, industry and intelligence their natural reward, idleness and folly their natural punishment, by maintaining peace, by defending property, by diminishing the price of law, and by observing strict economy in every department of the state. Let the Government do this: the People will assuredly do the rest.

Fichte, Ruskin, Chamberlain, Gentile, and Eliot: Champions of Fascist Control

Most people are aware of the influence of Karl Marx and his ideological compatriots in building 20th-century totalitarianism. But there is another tradition of thought, dating from the early 19th century and continuing through the interwar period, that took a different route in coming to roughly the same conclusions regarding the place of the state in our lives.

As opposed to Marx's "left-Hegelians," these thinkers are part of the "right-Hegelian" movement who dispensed with the universalism of Marx to applaud nation, race, and war as the essence of life.

These thinkers also loathed commercial society and capitalism in particular. They saw enterprise as soulless and culturally destructive, lacking in the higher meaning that only centralization and planning could provide.

Instead of trying to create some mythical future based in some fantasy of a new socialist man, they sought to beat back capitalism by clinging to the old order of government power, privilege, hierarchy, nationalism, and racist control. Their imagined future looked like the pre-capitalist past they idealized.

These five thinkers appear in chronological order. In the prehistory of the alt-right, I mapped the big thinkers. Here we have some more minor and eccentric players in the evolution of an anti-capitalist right.

Johann Fichte (1762–1814) was the philosophical founder of German idealism, writing
and teaching a generation before George Friedrich
Hegel, and the first of a long line of obscurantist
philosophers whose ideas somehow land with one
solid political application: build a huge state led by
one heroic dictator. It was he, and not Hegel, who
first posited a meta-narrative of historical waves
that could be characterized as thesis, antithesis,
and synthesis.

In politics, he was a huge fan of Napoleon, but found himself
devastated by the crushing victory of France over German territories,
which motivated his "Addresses to the German Nation" (1808), the
most influential lecture series on education to appear in the modern
world. Here was the first complete outline of what German nationalism should look like.

The new education system should have "an absolutely new system
of German national education, such as has never existed in any other
nation." The purpose is to educate a "new race of men" with a system
that "must first be applied by Germans to Germans." Its goal is to incul-
cate "the true and all-powerful love of fatherland, the conception of our
people as an eternal people and as the security for our own eternity."

Part of the point is to train for work so that "no article of food,
clothing, etc., and, so far as this is possible, no tool is to be used, which
is not produced and made" inside Germany. In other words: autarky.
Germany should aspire to be "a closed commercial State" that rejects
"our idolatrous veneration of coined metals."

His template for what became fascist (right-Hegelian) thought
is entirely predictable: statism, nationalism, loathing of the merchant
class, and protectionism, spiced up with the inevitable doses of misogyny ("active citizenship, civic freedom and even property rights should
be withheld from women, whose calling was to subject themselves

utterly to the authority of their fathers and husbands") and anti-Semitism (granting rights to Jews requires we "cut off all their heads in one night, and to set new ones on their shoulders, which should contain not a single Jewish idea").

John Ruskin (1819–1900) is inexplicably revered to this day as an aesthete, artist, and champion of small crafts, whereas in truth he was an absolute hater of commercial capitalism, laissez faire liberalism, and the modern world. A hugely influential thinker of the Victorian period, he romanticized a mythic England from the past, in which art and good taste prevailed over commercial frenzy and wealth-making. "I was, and my father was before me, a violent Tory of the  old school," he said. In his view, he completely agreed with his friend Thomas Carlyle that the forces unleashed by Adam Smith and the Scottish Enlightenment generally had destroyed the artistic sensibilities of generations, and they needed to be recaptured through a strong planning state.

His most political book is *Unto This Last* (1862) which took aim at the division of labor itself. Riffing off the Parable of the Vineyards, he finds it outrageous that the vineyard owner himself was in a position to decide pay at all. The entire book is a long and tedious screed against merchants for their lack of loyalty, their obedience to impersonal market forces, and absence of a moral reason for existence. The merchant, he said, is "the man who does not know when to die, does not know how to live."

Like other critics of classical political economy (he compared it to "alchemy, astrology, witchcraft"), he denied that exchange alone could produce any value or profit. "It is only in labor there can be profit," he declared. He had a particular beef with John Stuart Mill, and critiqued his price and wage theory, showing near-zero competence in economic theory at all. For Ruskin, economics was not a science but an aesthetic. He summed up his outlook on political economy as follows: "Government and cooperation are in all things the laws of life; anarchy and competition the laws of death." It's no wonder that Ludwig von Mises said that Ruskin was "one of the gravediggers of British freedom, civilization and prosperity."

Houston Stewart Chamberlain (1855– 1927) is an exceedingly strange figure in the history of politics and ideas: a British-born German whose influence bled into Germany and back again to his home. As son-in-law to the famed composer Richard Wagner, he became a dear friend and fanatical admirer of Adolph Hitler and the most aggressive proponent of virulent anti-Semitism ever to come out of England.

He had decided early in life to locate the source of all political and economic evil in the Industrial Revolution, preferring his own made-up vision of what he called "Merry Old England" consisting of a beautiful aristocracy, hard-toiling and thrifty peasants, and patriotic citizens dedicated to preserving the language and race against the commercial forces of modernity. Under these conditions, unlike the demographic mess unleashed by capitalism, women were submissive to the wills of their fathers and husbands, devoted only to furthering the superior race.

His weird 1899 book *The Foundations of the Nineteenth Century* became a bestseller, many times over, throughout the Continent. Heavily influenced by the racial typologies that were increasingly popular, he described the Jews as mindlessly materialistic and the source of most evil in the modern world.

The Jews, he said, caused the downfall of Rome, for example. He argued that Jesus cannot possibly have been a Jew since all good in the world emanates from the pure Aryan race. Instead, he was "of exceptional beauty, tall and slim with a noble face inspiring respect and love; his hair blond shading into chestnut brown, his arms and hands noble and exquisitely formed." It was in this book that he laid out his theory that a Jewish plot was afoot to wipe out the Aryan race and turn all Europe into a race of "pseudo-Hebraic mestizos."

His book, which was printed in eight editions in the first ten years of its publication, and eventually sold as many as 250,000 copies by 1938, catapulted him into the status of a celebrity intellectual. And so his every utterance became gospel for his followers, even his proclamation that the Great War, which he believed the Jews had started, had led England "totally into the hands of the Jews and the Americans" and capitalist machinery.

It was in the midst of his fame that he reached out to an emergently powerful Hitler. Hearing that both Hitler and Joseph Goebbels could be counted among his fan base, he wrote Hitler in 1923:

> Most respected and dear Hitler ... It is hardly surprising that a man like that can give peace to a poor suffering spirit! Especially when he is dedicated to the service of the fatherland. My faith in Germandom has not wavered for a moment, though my hopes were— I confess—at a low ebb. With one stroke you have transformed the state of my soul. That Germany, in the hour of her greatest need, brings forth a Hitler—that is proof of her vitality ... I can now go untroubled to sleep ... May God protect you!

After Hitler's conviction of high treason following the Beerhall putsch, Chamberlain stuck by him and kept hope alive. Hitler was touched, and, following Hitler's release from prison, Hitler paid a visit to Chamberlain in Bayreuth in 1927, accompanied by Goebbels. Chamberlain assured Hitler that he was certainly "the chosen one," thereupon lifting Hitler's spirits. The leading Nazi in-house philosopher, Alfred Rosenberg, was perhaps an even greater fan of

Chamberlain. An ailing Chamberlain died in 1927, never knowing of the Nazi attempt to deal with the "Jewish problem" he had dedicated his life to exposing.

Giovanni Gentile (1874–1944) might be the most clownish and ridiculous of all the figures mentioned here, but he was a big shot in his time. He aspired to be the Marx of fascism, a leading theorist of the idealist tradition who finally put together the essential pieces of a thorough-going non-Marxist statism. His writings enjoyed some degree of fame in America in the interwar period, working on his own writings and ghost-writing for Benito Mussolini who was frequently solicited for American-published academic writings in the 1920s.

Most familiar to American readers was Gentile's 1922 book *The Reform of Education* published by Harcourt, Brace, and Company. The book contains the usual call for education to be compulsory, militarized, and nationalistic, rooted in a view of the heroic enterprise of nation building. For the most part, the book consists of pseudo-scholarly blather of the insufferably ponderous sort, but it does contain his theory of the state, as a kind of warm up to the educational material:

> A nation can under no circumstances exist prior to the form of its State ... a State is always a future. It is that state which this very day we must set up, or rather at this very instant, and with all our future effort bent to that political ideal which beams before us, not only in the light of a beautiful thought, but as the irresistible need of our own personality. The nation therefore is as intimately pertinent and native to our own being as the State, considered as Universal Will, is one with our concrete and actual ethical personality.

And so on for 250 pages. Despite the relentless statism of his vision, and his love of centralized power and planning, Gentile's writings lacked some features that characterized other works in this genre.

It is mercifully free of racism, perhaps because of his region of origin. He was Sicilian, and thereby belonged to a people who had been demonized by American thinkers as dysgenic since the 1880s. Indeed, if it is possible to talk this way, Gentile was a relative liberal among the fascists of the period, having criticized German anti-Semitism and having met his death at the hands of an anti-fascist mob having returned from arguing for the release of anti-fascists from prison.

Nonetheless, his signature contribution, signed by many Italian intellectuals, was the "Manifesto of the Fascist Intellectuals."

> The opposition of individual and State is the typical political expression of a corruption so deep that it cannot accept any higher life principle, because doing so would vigorously inform and contain the individual's feelings and thoughts. Fascism was, therefore, a political and moral movement at its origins. It understood and championed politics as a training ground for self-denial and self-sacrifice in the name of an idea, one which would provide the individuals with his reason for being, his freedom, and all his rights. The idea in question is that of the fatherland. It is an ideal that is a continuous and inexhaustible process of historical actualization. It represents a distinct and singular embodiment of a civilization's traditions which, far from withering as a dead memory of the past, assumes the form of a personality focused on the end towards which it strives. The fatherland is, thus, a mission.

Reading his brand of fascism, you can see why it went down easier with the American public than the English or German models. It was no more or less than the celebration of the state as the center of life, and a proclamation of the death of old-world freedom and democracy. In short, Gentile struck a chord in US political life for his description of the prevailing ethos of the New Deal itself.

T.S. Eliot (1888–1965) seems like an implausible candidate for inclusion in this gallery of rogues, simply because this paragon of civility and erudition is so widely championed in the annals of anti-liberalism. The American-born Anglophile is the author, after all, of the most famous and revered poem of the 20th century, "The Waste Land" (1922). Its impenetrable narrative captures the post-WWI despair of the English-speaking world, giving the impression that it was not only the war that civilization should regret but the whole of what life had become in the age of mass commerce. Nothing is salvageable, and everything is corrupt.

C.S. Lewis, who regarded Eliot's work as nothing short of "evil," said of this poem: "no man is fortified against chaos by reading the Wasteland, but that most men are by it infected with chaos." What is that chaos? It is the dark longing for some long-dead past and a conviction of the irredeemability of the present, an attitude which is anathema to the classical liberal tradition that sees hope and wonder in what freedom can achieve. It is not a stretch to see Eliot's literary contribution as part of the entire Modernist literary project in England to put down and condemn everything that capitalism had done for the world. For Eliot in particular, the cost was the integrity of culture itself.

In "Notes Toward a Definition of Culture," Eliot takes hard aim at the entire liberal/Hayekian view of culture as a spontaneous evolution extending from the gradual emergence of norms, tastes, and manner of a free people. For Eliot, the right kind of culture must emanate from an elite, chosen from excellent educational institutions. Everything about industrialization wars against culture, even the advances in publishing. "In our time," he declared, "we read too many new books... We are encumbered not only with too many new books: we are further embarrassed by too many periodicals, reports and privately circulated memoranda."

A growing amount of scholarship has taken Eliot to task for his sympathies for the Eugenics movement and his consistent worry about the rising birth rates among the lower classes in English culture. But this should not be surprising at all. It is but a small step from regretting the advance of mass consumerism to decrying the rise of mass population expansion made possible by prosperity.

In the end, the problem with Eliot is not nearly on the scale you find in the other writers in this tradition. He nowhere defends totalitarianism or anything like it, though you do pick up a hint of authoritarianism. But what he represents is an underlying problem that is universal among this strain of anti-capitalist writers.

The problem comes down to an intractably aristocratic snobbery that feeds a deep suspicion against freedom and tempts intellectuals to imagine that if we only constrained that freedom and replaced it with wise controls over our social, cultural, and demographic destiny, we might be saved from the decay and corruption into which the liberalism of the 18th century plunged us. Despots thrive off just such convictions.

The Fork in the Road

What you find in this tradition is a very different template from Marx and his school for criticizing the freely evolving society celebrated by the liberal tradition of Adam Smith and Frederic Bastiat. The non-Marxist version has no fundamental objection to religion, nation, family, and even property, provided everything is directed toward the single goal of fortifying the collective.

What they share in common is a conviction that the freely evolving commercial society is unsustainably corrupt; society does not contain within itself the capacity for its own self-ordering; and human relationships are not capable of achieving universal harmony absent conscious design by states, powerful leaders, and intellectuals.

Their vast influence over the bloody politics of the 20th century is strangely forgotten, and the tradition of thought they represent papered over during the Cold War, which rerendered the only political conflict as the West vs. Communism. The ideas of a rightist form of totalism was lying in wait for the moment to re-rear its ugly head.

Knowing this helps us understand the new politics of our time. Freedom is threatened from two ends, the right and left. The idea of liberty really does represent a third way, a path lit by the hope in the kind of civilization that can be built not from the top down but from the bottom up, not through the force of power but by voluntary associations of regular people who aspire to live better lives.

Thomas Carlyle, the Founding Father of Fascism

Have you heard of the "great man" theory of history?

The meaning is obvious from the words. The idea is that history moves in epochal shifts under the leadership of visionary, bold, often ruthless men who marshall the energy of masses of people to push events in radical new directions. Nothing is the same after them.

In their absence, nothing happens that is notable enough to qualify as history: no heroes, no god-like figures who qualify as "great." In this view, we need such men. If they do not exist, we create them. They give us purpose. They define the meaning of life. They drive history forward.

Great men, in this view, do not actually have to be fabulous people in their private lives. They need not exercise personal virtue. They need not even be moral. They only need to be perceived as such by the masses, and play this role in the trajectory of history.

Such a view of history shaped much of historiography as it was penned in the late 19th century and early 20th century, until the revisionists of the last several decades saw the error and turned instead to celebrate private life and the achievements of common folk instead. Today the "great man" theory history is dead as regards academic history, and rightly so.

Carlyle the Proto-Fascist

The originator of the great man theory of history is British philosopher Thomas Carlyle (1795–1881), one of the most revered thinkers of his day. He also coined the expression "dismal science" to describe the economics of his time. The economists of the day, against whom he constantly inveighed, were almost universally champions of the free market, free trade, and human rights.

His seminal work on "great men" is *On Heroes, Hero-Worship, and the Heroic in History* (1840). This book was written to distill his entire worldview.

Considering Carlyle's immense place in the history of 19th century intellectual life, this is a surprisingly nutty book. It can clearly be seen as paving the way for the monster dictators of the 20th century. Reading his description of "great men" literally, there is no sense in which Mao, Stalin, and Hitler—or any savage dictator from any country you can name—would not qualify.

Indeed, a good case can be made that Carlyle was the forefather of fascism. He made his appearance in the midst of the age of laissez faire, a time when the UK and the US had already demonstrated the merit of allowing society to take its own course, undirected from the top down. In these times, kings and despots were exercising ever less control and markets ever more. Slavery was on its way out. Women obtained rights equal to men. Class mobility was becoming the norm, as were long lives, universal opportunity, and material progress.

Carlyle would have none of it. He longed for a different age. His literary output was devoted to decrying the rise of equality as a norm and calling for the restoration of a ruling class that would exercise firm and uncontested power for its own sake. In his view, some were meant to rule and others to follow. Society must be organized hierarchically lest his ideal of greatness would never again be realized. He set himself up as the prophet of despotism and the opponent of everything that was then called liberal.

Right Authoritarianism of the 19th Century

Carlyle was not a socialist in an ideological sense. He cared nothing for the common ownership of the means of production. Creating an ideologically driven social ideal did not interest him at all. His writings appeared and circulated alongside those of Karl Marx and his contemporaries, but he was not drawn to them.

Rather than an early "leftist," he was a consistent proponent of power and a raving opponent of classical liberalism, particularly of the legacies of Adam Smith and John Stuart Mill. If you have the slightest leanings toward liberty, or affections for the impersonal forces of markets, his writings come across as ludicrous. His interest was in power as the central organizing principle of society.

Here is his description of the "great men" of the past:

> They were the leaders of men, these great ones; the modellers, patterns, and in a wide sense creators, of whatsoever the general mass of men contrived to do or to attain; all things that we see standing accomplished in the world are properly the outer material result, the practical realization and embodiment, of Thoughts that dwelt in the Great Men sent into the world: the soul of the whole world's history....

> One comfort is, that Great Men, taken up in any way, are profitable company. We cannot look, however imperfectly, upon a great man, without gaining something by him. He is the living light-fountain, which it is good and pleasant to be near. The light which enlightens, which has enlightened the darkness of the world; and this not as a kindled lamp only, but rather as a natural luminary shining by the gift of Heaven; a flowing light-fountain, as I say, of native original insight, of manhood and heroic nobleness;—in whose radiance all souls feel that it is well with them. ...

> Could we see them well, we should get some glimpses
> into the very marrow of the world's history. How
> happy, could I but, in any measure, in such times as
> these, make manifest to you the meanings of Heroism;
> the divine relation (for I may well call it such) which in
> all times unites a Great Man to other men...

And so on it goes for hundreds of pages that celebrate "great" events such as the Reign of Terror in the aftermath of the French Revolution (one of the worst holocausts then experienced). Wars, revolutions, upheavals, invasions, and mass collective action, in his view, were the essence of life itself. The merchantcraft of the industrial revolution, the devolution of power, the small lives of the bourgeoisie all struck him as noneventful and essentially irrelevant. These marginal improvements in the social sphere were made by the "silent people" who don't make headlines and therefore don't matter much; they are essential at some level but inconsequential in the sweep of things.

To Carlyle, nothing was sillier than Adam Smith's pin factory: all those regular people intricately organized by impersonal forces to make something practical to improve people's lives. Why should society's productive capacity be devoted to making pins instead of making war? Where is the romance in that?

Carlyle established himself as the arch-opponent of liberalism—heaping an unrelenting and seething disdain on Smith and his disciples. And what should replace liberalism? What ideology? It didn't matter, so long as it embodied Carlyle's definition of "greatness."

No Greatness Like the State

Of course there is no greatness to compare with that of the head of state.

> The Commander over Men; he to whose will our
> wills are to be subordinated, and loyally surrender
> themselves, and find their welfare in doing so, may

be reckoned the most important of Great Men. He is practically the summary for us of all the various figures of Heroism; Priest, Teacher, whatsoever of earthly or of spiritual dignity we can fancy to reside in a man, embodies itself here, to command over us, to furnish us with constant practical teaching, to tell us for the day and hour what we are to do.

Why the state? Because within the state, all that is otherwise considered immoral, illegal, unseemly, and ghastly, can become, as blessed by the law, part of policy, civic virtue, and the forward motion of history. The state baptizes rampant immorality with the holy water of consensus. And thus does Napoleon come in for high praise from Carlyle, in addition to the tribal chieftains of Nordic mythology. The point is not what the "great man" does with his power so much as that he exercises it decisively, authoritatively, ruthlessly.

The exercise of such power necessarily requires the primacy of the nation state, and hence the protectionist and nativist impulses of the fascist mindset.

Consider the times in which Carlyle wrote. Power was on the wane, and humankind was in the process of discovering something absolutely remarkable: namely, the less society is controlled from the top, the more the people thrive in their private endeavors. Society needs no management but rather contains within itself the capacity for self organization, not through the exercise of the human will as such, but by having the right institutions in place. Such was the idea of liberalism.

Liberalism was always counterintuitive. The less society is ordered, the more order emerges from the ground up. The freer people are permitted to be, the happier the people become and the more meaning they find in the course of life itself. The less power that is given to the ruling class, the more wealth is created and dispersed among everyone. The less a nation is directed by conscious design, the more it can provide a model of genuine greatness.

Such teachings emerged from the liberal revolution of the previous two centuries. But some people (mostly academics and would-be rulers) weren't having it. On the one hand, the socialists would not tolerate what they perceived to be the seeming inequality of the emergent commercial society. On the other hand, the advocates of old-fashioned ruling-class control, such as Carlyle and his proto-fascist contemporaries, longed for a restoration of pre-modern despotism, and devoted their writings to extolling a time before the ideal of universal freedom appeared in the world.

The Dismal Science

One of the noblest achievements of the liberal revolution of the late 18th and 19th centuries—in addition to the idea of free trade— was the movement against slavery and its eventual abolition. It should not surprise anyone that Carlyle was a leading opponent of the abolitionist movement and a thoroughgoing racist. He extolled the rule of one race over another, and resented especially the economists for being champions of universal rights and therefore opponents of slavery.

As David Levy has demonstrated, the claim that economics was a "dismal science" was first stated in an essay by Carlyle in 1848, an essay in which non-whites were claimed to be non-human and worthy of killing. Blacks were, to his mind, "two-legged cattle," worthy of servitude for all times.

Carlyle's objection to economics as a science was very simple: it opposed slavery. Economics imagined that society could consist of people of equal freedoms, a society without masters and slaves. Supply and demand, not dictators, would rule. To him, this was a dismal prospect, a world without "greatness."

The economists were the leading champions of human liberation from such "greatness." They understood, through the study of market forces and the close examination of the on-the-ground reality of factories and production structures, that wealth was made by the small actions of men and women acting in their own self interest. Therefore, concluded the economists, people should be free of despotism. They should be free to accumulate wealth. They should pursue their own interests in their own way. They should be let alone.

Carlyle found the whole capitalist worldview disgusting. His loathing foreshadowed the fascism of the 20th century: particularly its opposition to liberal capitalism, universal rights, and progress.

Fascism's Prophet

Once you get a sense of what capitalism meant to humanity—universal liberation and the turning of social resources toward the service of the common person—it is not at all surprising to find reactionary intellectuals opposing it tooth and nail. There were generally two schools of thought that stood in opposition to what it meant to the world: the socialists and the champions of raw power that later came to be known as fascists. In today's parlance, here is the left and the right, both standing in opposition to simple freedom.

Carlyle came along at just the right time to represent that reactionary brand of power for its own sake. His opposition to emancipation and writings on race would emerge only a few decades later into a complete ideology of eugenics that would later come to heavily inform 20th century fascist experiments. There is a direct line, traversing only a few decades, between Carlyle's vehement anti-capitalism and the ghettos and gas chambers of the German total state.

Do today's neo-fascists understand and appreciate their 19th century progenitor? Not likely. The continuum from Carlyle to Mussolini to Franco to Donald Trump is lost on people who do not see beyond the latest political crisis. Not one in ten thousand activists among the European and American "alt-right" who are rallying around would-be strong men who seek power today have a clue about their intellectual heritage.

And it should not be necessary that they do. After all, we have a more recent history of the rise of fascism in the 20th century from which to learn (and it is to their everlasting disgrace that they have refused to learn).

But no one should underestimate the persistence of an idea and its capacity to travel time, leading to results that no one intended directly but are still baked into the fabric of the ideological structure. If you celebrate power for its own sake, herald immorality as a civic ideal, and believe that history rightly consists of nothing more than the brutality of great men with power, you end up with unconscionable results that may not have been overtly intended but which were nonetheless given license by the absence of conscious opposition.

As time went on, left and right mutated, merged, diverged, and established a revolving door between the camps, disagreeing on the ends they sought but agreeing on the essentials. They would have opposed 19th-century liberalism and its conviction that society should be left alone. Whether they were called socialist or fascists, the theme was the same. Society must be planned from the top down. A great man—brilliant, powerful, with massive resources at his disposal—must lead. At some point in the middle of the 20th century, it became difficult to tell the difference but for their cultural style and owned constituencies. Even so, left and right maintained distinctive forms. If Marx was the founding father of the socialist left, Carlyle was his foil on the fascist right.

Hitler and Carlyle

In his waning days, defeated and surrounded only by loyalists in his bunker, Hitler sought consolation from the literature he admired the most. According to many biographers, the following scene took place. Hitler turned to Goebbels, his trusted assistant, and asked for a final reading. The words he chose to hear before his death were from Thomas Carlyle's biography of Frederick the Great. Thus did Carlyle himself provide a fitting epitaph to one of the "great" men he so celebrated during his life: alone, disgraced, and dead.

The Brooding Baron
of 20th-Century Fascism

The history of fascist ideology extends from the early 19th century through our own times: from Fichte to Hegel to Carlyle to List to Ruskin to Spengler toGrant to Spann to Gentile to Schmitt and (skipping a half century) finally to thousands of meme-posting sock puppets on Twitter. These thinkers are united in their loathing of capitalism but also opposition to communism, which is the feature of their identity that is considered right-wing.

Things were never as weird with this camp as during the interwar period, particularly among the intellectuals (or pseudo-intellectuals) that rallied political movements toward violence and state centralization. The main thinkers in this tradition had been largely forgotten until their relatively recent revival in European and American politics. They had unmistakable and consistent ideological traits. They were socialists (and nationalists) who decried capitalism as decadent anomy, but railed against communism too, on grounds that it was too universalist and deracinating of the people's identity.

The far left and far right have long shared in common the view that social harmony is an illusory ideal concocted by the liberal tradition. Whereas the Marxists divide society by class, the fascists divided society by religion, race, language, geography, and lineage. They favored strong-man politics, dabbled in pseudo-science and occultism, and never tired of predicting doom for civilization. Above all else, they despised bourgeois liberalism, probably even more then they hated communism.

Who was the strangest among them? There is tough competition for that title. Could it be Francis Parker Yockey, the one-time American leftist who became a frenzied champion of Hitler: whose delirious "masterwork" *Imperium* has inspired several generations of hardcore anti-Semites? Or perhaps it is George Lincoln Rockwell, the founder of the American Nazi Party who believed that one-man dictatorship was the only hope to rescue America from the Jews and non-whites who inhabited the same nation as the master race?

The Baron

My vote is for the oddest bird among them (and that's saying something), and perhaps the most interesting: the monocle-wearing Baron Giulio Cesare Andrea Evola (1898–1974), better known as Julius Evola. Always cagey about his background and education, his followers believed him to be of Sicilian aristocratic lineage, a real-life noble in their midst who was an inexhaustible font of wisdom. Benito Mussolini as well as many Nazi party officials—even the Fuhrer himself—were taken in by his strange brew of dialectical apocalypticism, violent misogyny, Jew hating, and longing for global war to restore the golden age of the warrior class.

Truly, reading his works—I do not recommend it for the faint-of-heart—is a tour of a mind put several times through a blender of malicious nonsense from the first to the last. His thought contains all the usual fascist tropes, but takes them to a new level of faux-erudition and philosophical frenzy.

Who Was Evola?

Julius Evola was born in Rome in 1898 and studied engineering briefly in college before deciding that the discipline was too bourgeois for him; he didn't want conventional credentials in any case. Like so many others of his generation, his life was interrupted by the Great War, which unleashed a bloody nihilism in Europe, particularly among the artistically inclined.

Following the war, he threw himself into art and philosophy, driving himself toward radical antiliberalism and anti-Catholicism. In this, he was not unlike so many displaced minor nobles of his time. Alienated by democracy and robbed of social position by the pace of modern life, but absolutely unwilling to hold a regular job, he turned to hard-core reactionary politics in a longing to wipe out the modern world and turn it back to some imagined ancient manly despotism.

The Devil

He came to public attention with his first major work, *Pagan Imperialism* (1928), a massive attack on the Catholic Church, on grounds that the Pope and the Bishops as power had displaced the more legitimate source of moral and legal authority of the imperial state, which he, like everyone else in this right-Hegelian tradition, believed was the central authority of history's trajectory. To him (again predictably), Christianity was feminized, egalitarian, humanitarian, weak, and excessively pro-peace, and so the Church had to be smashed if civilization were to be saved.

The Catholic Church was mortified by the attack (the Vatican called him the "Italian Satan") and his book became a huge subject of debate in intellectual circles where fascists and communists battled it out all over Europe. Among the participants was the man who would later become Pope Paul VI (who presided over the Second Vatican

Council in the early 1960s), who might have believed that the only way to protect Europe against violent fascism was through a turn to the left.

Heart of Darkness

Like all fascist intellectuals of the interwar period, Evola wrote extensively on the race issue, and, given the context of the time, his views were slightly more liberal than, for example, the doctrinaire Nazis. He believed that the human person was made of biology, mind, and spirit, so that a person could be a Jew biologically but an Aryan in mind and therefore not entirely intolerable. That Evola was considered a heretic by the hard-core Nazis tells you all you need to know about these times and the strange ideas extant in European intellectual circles.

During Mussolini's consolidation of power in Italy, Evola became his biggest champion and admirer and came to cheer the most reactionary/totalitarian elements in European politics at the time. This culminated in his "magnum opus" called *Revolt Against the Modern World*. This book became an important rallying treatise of the reactionary movements in Italy, Spain, and Germany, standing alongside even *Mein Kampf* as an ideological justification for war and slaughter.

What does this book say? No surprise, he goes full Hegelian, positing a Golden Age of racial purity and perfect political organization that was disrupted by the advent of liberalism, but predicting that the decline will be ended by a full revolt in favor of a strongman-led state that will take us to a new era of perfect order. Of course, the book is thoroughly statist, thoroughly racist, massively opposed to every single improvement in living standards since the Age of the Enlightenment. It is a full-bore attack on human liberty itself.

I would quote it but most of it makes no sense, but you are welcome to a sample or to read the whole book. His central political conclusion is to favor the "establishment of order from above."

> The very notion of "natural rights" is a mere fiction,
> and the antitraditional and subversive use of that is

well documented. There is no such thing as a nature that is "good" in itself and in which the inalienable rights of an individual, which are to be equally enjoyed by every human being, are preformed and rooted. Even when the ethnic substance appears to be somewhat 'well defined'.... These forms...do not have a spiritual value in and of themselves unless participating in a higher order, such as when they are assumed in the state or an analogous traditional organization, they are first consecrated as being from above.

(Quoting Evola is always difficult because of his studied obscurantism, but I hope the reader gets the main drift.)

The Girl Problem

In this treatise, Evola presents his position on women, which he would revisit throughout a long literary writing career. Evola not only rejected any human rights for the half of the human race identified as women; he believed that the biological capacity to bear children mandates a situation of permanent slavery for women. His vision of the proper place of woman is represented by the captive harem during life and on the funeral pyre after the death of her master.

It is not possible, he wrote, for a society that grants "every human being" things such as "dignity" and "rights" to "preserve some sense of the correct relationship between the two sexes." He explains in an oddly clear passage:

In a society that no longer understands the figure of the ascetic and of the warrior; in which the hands of the latest aristocrats seem better fit to hold tennis rackets or shakers for cocktail mixes than swords or scepters; in which the archetype of the virile man is represented by the boxer or by a movie star if not by the dull wimp represented by the intellectual, the

college professor, the narcissistic puppet of the artist, or the busy and dirty money-making banker and
the politician—in such a society it was only a matter
of time before women rose up and claimed for themselves a "personality" and a "freedom" according to the
anarchist and individualist meaning usually associated
with those words.

In Evola's view, the emancipation of women in the 19th century
(the age of liberalism), combined with rising prosperity for everyone,
led to an intolerable demographic chaos. In his view, birth ought to be
regulated, mandated among the superior races (and that includes rape
as a moral imperative) but forbidden among the inferior races. If the
state doesn't get involved, humanity is absolutely doomed (a conventional claim of every eugenicist of his generation), so long as we continue to tolerate things like freedom and human rights.

It is no wonder the superior races are dying out before
the ineluctable logic of individualism, which especially in the so-called contemporary "higher classes,"
has caused people to lose all desire to procreate. Not
to mention all the other degenerative factors connected to a mechanized and urbanized social life and
especially to a civilization that no longer respects the
health and creative limitations constituted by the
castes and by the traditions of blood lineage. Thus proliferation is concentrated in the lower social classes
and in the inferior races where the animal-like impulse
is stronger than any rational calculation and consideration. The unavoidable effects are a reversed selection
and the ascent and the onslaught of inferior elements
against which the "race" of superior castes and people, now exhausted and defeated, can do very little as a
spiritually dominating element.

He ends this 1934 treatise with a blood-thirsty template for holocaust and the creation of a new man:

> This is all we can say about a certain category of men
> in view of the fulfillment of the times, a category that
> by virtue of its own nature must be that of a minority.
> This dangerous path may be trodden. It is a real test. In
> order for it to be complete in its resolve it is necessary
> to meet the following conditions: all the bridges are
> to be cut, no support found, and no returns possible;
> also, the only way out must be forward. It is typical of
> a heroic vocation to face the greatest wave knowing
> that two destinies lie ahead: that of *those who will die*
> with the dissolution of the modern world, and that of
> *those who will find themselves in the main and regal
> stream* of the new current.

His subsequent flurry of literature, through the rest of the 1930s
leading to the Second World War, included reconstructions of early
pre-modern history in which every time the merchant prevailed over
the warlords, commerce and harmony replaced rape and pillage, Evola
cries foul. Humanity lost its love of bloodshed and horror and therefore the essence of life itself!

You read enough of this stuff and it all becomes absurdly predictable. Liberty in all its forms is the enemy; hatred, tribal violence, dictatorship, mythological love of the lie, is the philosophical aspiration of
superior people. Though Evola's books poured out in the years before
the war, each was a variation on the same theme.

Dalliance with the Nazis

As the Nazi party made advances in German politics, Evola was
enraptured, placing all his hopes and dreams into the great cause, and
became a full-time propagandist working in Germany. He spoke on
behalf of the Third Reich, and became good friends with Nazi official

and extermination-camp builder Heinrich Himmler. His services were so appreciated that Evola eventually became a top intellectual in Nazi circles, a genuine intellectual insider of a cause who provided ideological cover for its crimes, while cheering every aspect of Hitler's war and regime as the best possible hope for humanity. He even ended up escorting Mussolini to Hitler's hideout during the war. Evidently, the slaughter of innocents was not only just fine by him but embodied some realization of what he believed must happen.

So worshipful did Evola become of violence and death that he made it a habit to walk around Mussolini's short-lived Social Republic, contemplating the spiritual meaning of bombs, during which time he was hit by a shell that left him paralyzed. His disability only added to his mystique after the war during which time he cheered the violent juntas that held out for a fascist utopia even following Allied victories. Evola ended up escaping prosecution after the war, most likely by cleverly boring the jury with abstruse philosophical ramblings.

The writings from his last years demonstrate that he never gave up his faith in fascist revolution. His 1974 book *Fascism as Viewed from the Right* downplayed some of his weird views on sex and race but reiterated the main theme: statism as a replacement for classical liberalism.

> The true state will be oriented against both capitalism and communism. At its center will stand a principle of authority and a transcendent symbol of sovereignty.... The state is the primary element that precedes nation, people, and society. The state—and with the state everything that is properly constituted as political order and political reality—is defined essentially on the basis of an idea, not by naturalistic and contractual factors.

Paradise Lost

Baron Evola was hardly singular in his outlook among his class. At the end of the 19th century, there were many such minor nobles who felt stranded in the age of democracy, loose in the world, brilliant and privileged but unwilling to get a conventional education much less take a regular job. World War I shattered their moral lineage, so many turned to outright nihilism out of anger at their personal plight. They also happened to be the smartest person in the room and they knew it.

What to do? Where to go? Basically, many of these people became The Joker, people who wanted to see the modern world burn. The world they knew they despised. But Mussolini was hope. Hitler was hope. The determined strongman, the use of massive force to turn back history, the extermination camp, and the eventual gas chamber: these were hope. These displaced minds couldn't fight but they could think, lecture, and write. They wrote treatises on why mass death was the source of life. They went from one-time angels of old Europe to Satans in the new, as the Vatican said of Evola. And today? Their legacy lives on, tragically and horribly.

So that I'm clear: I'm not unsympathetic with their personal plight. Everyone has a reason for how he or she is. But the fact is that they used their gifts for evil, and are full accomplices in bringing it about.

The Lure of Gnosticism

Why are people drawn to the views of such thinkers? Why are Evola's works newly translated and selling again? Why is there Juliusevola.com?

You could theorize that this is what you get when the left goes too far; it creates a radical right as a mirror image. That might be a factor. More fundamentally, however, Eric Voegelin is right: it has to do with the attraction of a secret teaching, the great Gnostic appeal, stemming

from an initial distrust of conventional learning and wisdom and leading to a search for some lost and suppressed worldview.

People like Baron Evola have a special attraction for such people
because of their supposed aristocratic lineage; this hints of the master's alienation from prevailing corruption and signals the possibility
of truthful revelation, some hidden truth buried in the great mind. It's
all the better when people like this write treatises of a thousand pages
that reconstruct the story of humankind in super un-PC terms, placing blame for the loss of greatness on invaders, deviants, feminization,
almost always the Jews, or some other supposed artificial turn that
leads humankind away from its organic destiny to be led by mighty
men (and the readers of such books always imagine themselves to be
among them).

There seems to be some sneaky pleasure in pouring over such dark
works, like a sin against a corrupt and expendable society. For followers of such thinkers, that the books don't make much sense is hardly
the point. What matters most is that the author himself represents
isolation, exclusion, condemnation, and his works are suppressed by
prevailing elites. It is the very rejection of their thought by the establishment that is the source of their power among people afflicted with
such Gnostic longings.

Evola Lives

Every reactionary ideology—every outlook on life that harbors
deep resentment against the liberation of humanity from deprivation
and barbarism—has a vision of an idealized past, a theory of its decline
and fall, and a plan for restoration which is necessarily violent. The fascist movements of the interwar period became the flypaper for all these
activists in Europe.

The pompous and ridiculous Baron Giulio Cesare Andrea
Evola, whose works, to this very day, entice alienated and authoritarian pseudo-intellectuals around the world, lives on through his works

translated in at least five languages. His thought—like the writings of medieval occultists—will most likely attract brooding and bitter autodidacts around the world for decades to come. Both Steve Bannon and Milo Yiannopoulos have cited Evola as inspiration.

And the biggest irony of all: Evola's ideas are only accessible today due to the very technology—and ideals behind that technology—that he dedicated his life to opposing. Ludwig von Mises has the last word: "fascism is not as the Fascists trumpeted a 'new way to life'; it is a rather old way towards destruction and death."

We Fight to Feel Alive

"I'm just here for violence."

So read a sign by a man in New Orleans protesting the city's decision to remove some marbled tributes to the Confederacy.

This seems to be a growing tendency around the country. Is there a controversial speaker coming to campus? Let's go and be disruptive or disrupt the disrupters. Is there a pro-Trump or anti-Trump rally happening? Let go and see if we can partake in some fisticuffs. Which side should we choose? That matters, but not as much as the appeal of the clash itself. Conflict, even violence, makes us feel alive.

On the digital level, we've all been dragged into wicked flame wars on every platform, where small differences of opinion devolve quickly to insult to viciousness to blocking. Twitter has become the haven for provocateurs to demonize, threaten, and swear retribution upon others. Every public intellectual today faces some degree of harassment on this level.

The longing for a fight isn't just an American problem. It affects every European country, where political groups are going to their corners and coming out swinging.

The Fight Club

Sometimes a movie can be so far ahead of its time that we forget how much it foreshadowed. So I'm not entirely sad that I waited until 2017 to see the 1999 classic movie *Fight Club*. I didn't know the story and had no expectations, much less any notion of the plot twist. This is the best way to experience the film. It did to me exactly what it was meant to do: take me on a long journey from the mundane to beyond-belief absurdism.

The film is a creation of the legendary David Fincher, based on the book by the same name by Chuck Palahniuk. It stars Edward Norton as the mild-mannered narrator, Brad Pitt as the tough-talking guru of the club Tyler Durden, and Helena Bonham Carter as the disheveled but beautiful Marla Singer. There are three distinct stages to the plot's development, but the main one involves the creation of a club for boys to beat each other senseless, just because it makes them feel good.

They gather in an appointed spot at an appointed time and start throwing punches until one person says enough. It's not about anger. It's not even about winning. It's about discovering something about yourself: the pain you can feel and the pain you can inflict, which is somehow more real than anything else in your life. It connects to a primal side of us that we've lost in the course of betting and prettifying our lives while actually draining away our core bio-evolutionary drive to struggle.

As a viewer, you are aghast, but the case for the practice is also strangely compelling. One of the main criticisms of the movie when it came out was that the whole notion was actually too compelling. Reviewers didn't doubt the quality of the movie, but they were very worried about whether the narrative would create copycat clubs and behavior around the world.

Remember, this was 1999. We had no notion then of the Alt-right or the Antifa. ISIS, Trump, Sanders, and the rise of mega-toxic online culture was nowhere in sight. The income stagnation of young white men didn't become entrenched until after 2008. The cultural trope of middle-class people looking for meaning and growing tired of merely consuming is more of our time than the last century. And the general sense of a slow-growth economic environment festering and leading to longing for violence had not emerged. The final scene with collapsing buildings eerily foreshadows 9/11.

The connection to our times is obvious, with the growing street battles between left and right, the winning of which decides nothing but makes the participants feel as if they matter. Indeed, the movie was truly before its time.

Seeing the Future

This movie is nearly spooky with regard to how much of the future it managed to anticipate. Made at the end of the second millennium it seems to anticipate a return of brutalism in the third millennium. Though it tells the story of a just a few people, gradually morphing into a tale of gang organization and violence, it serves as a prescient allegory for the rise of a new form of politics in the 21st century.

The movie begins with the feel of a light comedy. A young man with a white collar job busies himself filling up his apartment with Ikea furniture and defining his lifestyle with careful choices over glassware. He has to travel often for his business, and it has become routine to him. Nothing particularly meaningful or interesting ever happens. He has developed insomnia and seeks out some cure for it, but nothing seems to work.

One day, on an airline flight, our narrator meets Tyler Durden, who seems to be the most interesting person he has encountered in years. They meet up again later and the narrator stays at Tyler's house, which turns out to be a dilapidated mansion of sorts. Clowning around one day, Tyler insists that his new friend punch him. He does and Tyler punches back. A brawl ensues but instead of becoming enemies, they discover a source of friendship. It makes them feel like they are living large. "Quit your job. Start a fight. Prove you're alive," says Tyler. "If you don't claim your humanity, you will become a statistic."

The Rationale

The Fight Club grows and grows, and at some point, Tyler explains the underlying theory.

> Man, I see in fight club the strongest and smartest men who've ever lived. I see all this potential, and I see squandering. Damn it, an entire generation pumping gas, waiting tables; slaves with white collars. Advertising has us chasing cars and clothes, working jobs we hate so we can buy [stuff] we don't need. We're the middle children of history, man. No purpose or place. We have no Great War. No Great Depression. Our Great War's a spiritual war... our Great Depression is our lives. We've all been raised on television to believe that one day we'd all be millionaires, and movie gods, and rock stars. But we won't. And we're slowly learning that fact. And we're very, very pissed off.

We fight because we have no purpose, no place. To find them, the Fight Club shoves aside all things people associate with civilized behavior and reveals our inner manhood, our ability to feel and inflict pain. We need to see the blood to really believe in life.

The movie features over-the-top displays of masculine derring-do. The gendered element of the underlying philosophy is unmissable: contrasting civilization with manhood, as if peacefully cooperating with others for mutual gain in productive pursuits is a feminized undertaking, activities that are morally and physically emasculating. Men are born to fight and rule, not trade and cooperate, or so the theory goes.

There is a grain of truth here. The struggle, the fight, the kill, is the dominant story of humankind's existence, during which time male dominance and female subjugation were unquestioned. Women as a sex only gained the fullest possibility to exercise their human rights in the age of laissez-faire, the 19th-century belle epoch of peace, new technology, and commercial achievement, a time when the blood feud, the ethnic conflict, the race and religious war were at a low ebb, while manners, etiquette, and civilized deference to the well-being of others was on the rise.

Drama Lost and Regained

The idea of the Fight Club is to recapture the lost drama, drive, and sense of purpose that we can only experience through violence, according to countless champions of war from Carlyle to Schmitt. Following the onset of the Great Depression, the rise of fascist ideology in America and Europe had the same idea: effeminate ideas like peace and freedom didn't work, so let's try something masculine like power and war. Through them, we can recapture honor, discover what heroism looks like, strengthen our spirits, find out the meaning of greatness.

Is this really what war does? It can be associated with heroism in individual cases, but the main result is to unleash unthinkable horror. Indeed, as Christopher Hedges says in his classic 2002 work *War Is the Force that Gives Us Meaning*: war actually "exposes the capacity for evil that lurks not far below the surface within all of us." It is not manly but animalistic, not civilized but barbaric, not true but riven with lies.

In some sense, the Fight Club puts on display the most powerful critique of liberalism ever penned, the notion that peace, trade, and mutual cooperation, and the resulting social order of commercial production and consumption, robs our lives of drama and meaning. This can only be recaptured through the reassertion of the friends/enemies paradigm, and this, in turn, can only be made present in our lives through the fight. The film sets up this critique and then knocks it down beautifully by revealing it as a dangerous pathology that threatens us all.

It makes perfect sense, then, that the contemporary political Fight Club, though defined as right and left, and seemingly warring from opposite sides of the political spectrum, are absolutely united in one central point: opposition to the idea of peace and trade as pillars of the social order. The more you look, the more you realize that socialism and fascism, Alt-right and Antifa, far right and far left, have more in common than they like to admit.

As with the Fight Club itself, the purpose of the opposing sides in the modern political struggle is to find meaning through the fight itself. But a closer look reveals something remarkable: the opposites sides in the fight are really on the same team, and might even be the same person. How much difference, really, is there between the Hegelian of the right and the Hegelian of the left?

The foreign policy analogy has the US supporting both sides in Syria, bombing US-built tunnels in Afghanistan, and providing arms to both sides in civil wars around the world. What seems to be two sides, on closer inspection, turn out to be one side united in the love of struggle for its own sake. How else to explain the desire of the Trump administration to once again ramp up the fight in Afghanistan, a fight with no end in sight, and, to that extent, the model war for any cause that has given up belief in civilization itself?

But What about Drama?

What about this critique itself? Is the free society really devoid of drama? A contrasting view of this question comes from Ayn Rand's *Atlas Shrugged*, a book that departs from Scottish Enlightenment aesthetics to embrace a more Nietzschean spirit regarding enterprise. It is about discovery, competition, achievement, the tragedy of loss and the elation of triumph, all in the context of market exchange.

To my mind, this is the book's singular and epic achievement. It demonstrated that all the supposed honors and glories of war are actually better realized through commerce. Enterprise, in Rand's view, is the Fight Club without violence and blood but with all the excitement, daring, and drama. The book is not to everyone's taste, but it does do an effective job in countering the critique of markets that they are stultifying and emasculating of the human spirit.

It is especially notable that Rand's heroes maintain their motivation and morality even in the face of tremendous adversity. They reject the means of violence on principle and fight for their freedom and rights by use of their minds and their capacity for heroic production, not destruction. They don't go to the alleyways and beat each other up to find the meaning of existence. Instead, they stand up for human rights and personal achievement, even in the midst of an economy in decline, with property rights under fire, with bureaucrats ruling the day.

No one can say that this story lacks drama. On the contrary, Rand finds the ultimate drama in the fight for freedom, peace, property, and capitalism. As for the choice of violence, it is the path of losers, people who have lost confidence in their own ability to compete, create, and add value to great project of life. Tellingly, Rand's real hero in the book in a woman, a fact which flips the narrative of commercial life as emasculated. Violence is, in fact, an act of despair in one's own capacity to achieve as a human being.

How can believers in these liberal ideals today resist the Fight Club mentality? As with Rand's heroic characters, we should be conscientious objectors in the wars of our time, whether hot or cold, in politics or the streets, large or small. We have no dog in this fight. As they beat each other to a bloody pulp, let us go forth boldly to build a civilized, inclusive, peaceful, and free world. That is a truly heroic struggle, and a thoroughly sound and sane way fully to feel alive.

V

THE FUTURE

The West Is a Portable Idea, Not Blood and Soil

Not everyone who goes around celebrating the achievements of The West and decrying its destruction is a true friend of freedom. We've known this since at least a century ago, when the acclaimed German historian Oswald Spengler wrote his magisterial tome *The Decline of the West* (1919).

The book goes on for 800 pages about the magnificence of Western arts, sciences, literature, and wealth, but that's not its thesis. The purpose of the treatise was to issue a dark warning: the West must be tribalized under a new Caesarism and fast, before the other mighty tribes of the world win the struggle for control.

The ideologies of Liberalism and Socialism are dead, Spengler wrote, as is the money-based economy, which is too thin and weak to enter the struggle for control of history. A new form of dictatorship, backed by a conscious vision and will of political masters leading the people, was necessary to seize the day.

Spengler's huge book was met with awesome public acclaim, but what did it presage? Look at interwar Europe and you see.

That Poland Speech

The book comes to mind because of Donald Trump's Poland's speech, which was sometimes beautiful and inspiring and others times strangely ominous. It took a few days, but it is gradually dawning on people that the speech scripted by policy adviser Stephen Miller was more than a recitation of the usual political bromides. It was a proposal to refocus the governing philosophy of the United States at a deep level, and instill an awareness of the unique identity and mission of what he repeatedly called "The West"—a term that hasn't had political resonance in decades.

The West, in the way the speech rendered it, is not merely an idea, but a people, a nation unto itself, united by great achievements, including triumphs in great conflicts. For example, the speech recounted the remarkable heroism of those who resisted the Nazis in the Warsaw Uprising of 1943, and went further to celebrate the more recent resistance to Soviet occupation.

The way he recounted this history was just marvelous and inspired the crowd to nonstop standing and cheering.

It further sought to forge a solidarity—even an identity—between Poland and the United States as a distinct thing called the West, which Trump very beautifully described thusly:

> There is nothing like our community of nations. The world has never known anything like our community of nations. We write symphonies. We pursue innovation. We celebrate our ancient heroes, embrace our timeless traditions and customs, and always seek to explore and discover brand-new frontiers. We reward brilliance. We strive for excellence, and cherish inspiring works of art that honor God. We treasure the rule of law and protect the right to free speech and free expression. We empower women as pillars of our society and of our success. We put faith and family, not

government and bureaucracy, at the center of our lives.
And we debate everything. We challenge everything.
We seek to know everything so that we can better
know ourselves.

I've written against so many of Trump's policies and behaviors, but
these words are stirring and true (as is much of Spengler's book) and it
is about time that someone said them in this generation. But note what
is distinct about his formulation. He took pains to say that these traits
belong to a certain "community of nations," a particular people united
behind a certain way of life.

Unlike his predecessors in office, he refused to describe these as
hallmarks of the human ideal, a universal longing, but rather centered
this outlook on a particular people—not the ideas that the people hold
(ideas can be ported anywhere) but somehow embedded in a certain
demographic.

Two Enemies

Trump further warned that the West was under profound threat
from two enemies: the overweening bureaucratic state and invasion from foreign ideology (radical Islam). To fight against these two
threats, Trump prescribed a new awareness of the uniqueness of the
Western tradition.

The fundamental question of our time is whether
the West has the will to survive. Do we have the confidence in our values to defend them at any cost? Do
we have enough respect for our citizens to protect our
borders? Do we have the desire and the courage to preserve our civilization in the face of those who would
subvert and destroy it?

This is a lot to unpack! Trump is positing an existential threat that
can only be met by a conscious identity awareness. And what does this
awareness lead to? A willingness to defend, a courage to fight, a desire

to survive. And for what? For a way of life that resides within a narrow range of the human experience. It is not universal.

This isn't just my interpretation. David French of *National Review* insightfully contrasts Trump's speech with speeches by Bush and Obama, and observes: Trump "located the values that other presidents have deemed universal squarely within a Western context, and he specifically rejected a universalism and moral equivalence."

French's article seems to represent many opinions on the right side of the political spectrum, in which people are fed up with feeling as if they need to apologize for the achievements of the West and should rather take pride in them. As French says, Trump takes pain to locate these achievements in history with a certain specific experience of a particular people, attached to a particular Judeo-Christian outlook.

And yet, there really is a difference between celebrating freedom and engaging in crude cultural chauvinism. There is a world of difference between the claim that freedom grows out of certain institutions ("the primordial thing," said Ludwig von Mises, is "the idea of freedom from the state") and claiming that it is rooted in blood and soil.

Where Is Freedom?

The blood-and-soil view of what makes civilization great is contradicted by our own eyes. The world today shows the success of freedom and rights in many cultures and among many peoples the world over. Markets exist everywhere on the planet. So do human rights and the rule of law. So do symphonies, great architecture, innovation, free speech, and art. Wherever people are given freedom from the state, they thrive.

For proof, look no further than the Index of Economic Freedom. Champions including Hong Kong, Singapore, Australia, Mauritius, United Arab Emirates, and Chile are spread across the globe and span many races. What they have in common is not blood, religion, geography, or language but that primordial thing, liberty.

It's one thing to observe that this thing we call The West was first to fully develop liberal ideas. This makes the idea of The West a matter of historical documentation and an indisputable fact. It's another thing entirely to postulate that they belong to a certain people by virtue of... what? This was the unspoken aspect of Trump's speech. What does he really mean? Is it religion, geography, great leaders, language, or... race perhaps?

Hearing Dog Whistles

The prospect that Trump's speech was really a cover for a darker agenda prompted Peter Beinart to declare that Trump's speech was nothing more than an exercise in political and racial paranoia. The West is clearly not a geographic designation as such, since "Poland is further east than Morocco. France is further east than Haiti. Australia is further east than Egypt. Yet Poland, France, and Australia are all considered part of The West. Morocco, Haiti, and Egypt are not."

If not geographic, what is it?

> Poland is largely ethnically homogeneous. So when a
> Polish president says that being Western is the essence
> of the nation's identity, he's mostly defining Poland
> in opposition to the nations to its east and south.
> America is racially, ethnically, and religiously diverse.
> So when Trump says being Western is the essence of
> America's identity, he's in part defining America in
> opposition to some of its own people. He's not speak-
> ing as the president of the entire United States. He's
> speaking as the head of a tribe.

Before rejecting Beinart's claims as the tirades of a left-wing race-baiter, consider that Trump's formulation of The West as a people and experience rather than an idea represents a significant departure from old liberal ideals. In particular, the speech adds a special tweak to the enlightenment ideals we attached to thinkers like Hume, Locke,

Smith, and Jefferson, funneling them through the lens of a tradition of thought that stands opposed to those ideals. What he is really proposing here is another form of identity politics that rejects universalism in fact and goal.

The Trouble with Universalism

To be sure, the cause of universal rights has been used as an excuse to violate those very rights. When Condoleezza Rice said that freedom and democracy belong to all, she was justifying the kind of nation building for which the Bush and Clinton administration were most known. What that policy leads to is not freedom in fact, much less democracy, but chaos of the sort we see in the war-torn nations of the Middle East. Universalism of that sort leads to imperialism.

That is the wrong kind of universalism. It imagines that since everyone has human rights, the most powerful nation should grant them good and hard, even if at the expense of the human rights of those chalked up as "collateral damage." The critique of this view is also right. Freedom grows from a cultural firmament, gradually, as an extension of the hearts of the people. It can't be imposed at the point of a gun, whether it is done by left-leaning neoliberals or right-leaning neoconservatives.

Many people who rally around Trump's ideas today have identified this very problem with universalist politics. But are they choosing the right replacement? There has to be some alternative to "universalist" imperialism other than protectionism, isolation, cultural chauvinism, and religio-racial supremacy.

The Real Liberal Alternative

As it happens, there is an alternative. It was once called liberalism and today is called classical liberalism or libertarianism. With regard to this problem, the doctrine can be summarized as follows: universal rights, locally enforced. It observes that the longing for freedom is a universal ideal but it warns against any attempt by government to use power, at the expense of freedom, to impose it.

With Tocqueville, it defers to the cultural traditions and folkways of a people, recognizing that there are infinite ways in which universal rights come to be embodied in real human experience. It is tolerant and respectful of them all. In the writings of Ludwig von Mises, this liberalism sees its realization in limits on state power, the freedom of expression and movement for all individuals, free trade, and peace and harmony among peoples and nations.

Liberalism of this sort does not rest on some dark Hegelian view of history in the form expressed by Oswald Spengler a century ago. A new Caesarism will not save The West but rather take from it its most defining characteristic: freedom of the individual from the state.

The New Moderates

Where does that leave those of us who can't rally around Trump's vision or those who despise that vision? Maybe that leaves us in an enviable position.

Jimmy Wales of Wikipedia made a passing remark at FEEcon that stuck with me. He has long been a student of F.A. Hayek's work and a solid libertarian. He says that these days, he feels less strident than ever before, for one simple reason. The right and left have become intensely partisan, unreasonable, internal, and vituperative in their tribal loyalties, and this is precisely what their leadership wants. They are two tribes fighting over the spoils of a corrupt and failing system. In this war, no one can win.

This has put Wales and many of us in the implausible position of feeling like moderates. We are able to talk sense with any reasonable person without changing our principles. A libertarian can be the most radically moderate person in the room.

The path forward is to drop the longing for a great and decisive tribal conflict and move toward a system of peace, prosperity, and social harmony for all. It's not about blood and soil. It's about the pursuit of happiness that is the right of all people.

The message that universal liberty needs no tribal strongman has never been more appealing, or more necessary.

Left-Wing Economics Is No Match for Alt-Right Resentment

The Democratic leadership, and its left-wing intellectual base, are feeling implausibly smug these days. They figure it this way: the Trump era is going to inspire a blowback. Trump will make a terrible mess, destabilize income security and health care access, and skew social power in favor of fat cats, and all of this will make people angry.

Then the Left will hold all the cards. They will say: told ya so. They will tap into populist impulses with their own plan for greatness, tacking further Left than Obama was willing to go. They offer up vast income guarantees, expanded economic regulation, a puffed-up welfare state, universal health care, a war on rich people like Trump, and then they rule, forever and ever, *saecula saeculorum*, amen.

They should rethink this. It's probably not going to work.

It is precisely in reaction to such policies, and the complex demographics of class and race resentment they give rise to, that hard Right movements rose in the US and Europe. There will be no mass regret for turning away from social-democratic policies. On the contrary, sticking to big-government economics will perpetuate far-Right rule here and abroad. The Left has to rethink, and fast, and it means raising fundamental questions about their economic orthodoxies.

Internal Critique

Don't take my word for it. This analysis actually comes from a solid article in the center-Left media site Vox, "Why Left-Wing Economics Is Not the Answer to Right-Wing Populism." Keep in mind that this was written by friends of the Left, and they are sending a serious warning: there is no evidence that tacking Left has any chance of succeeding.

> The problem is that a lot of data suggests that countries with more robust welfare states tend to have stronger far-right movements. Providing white voters with higher levels of economic security does not tamp down their anxieties about race and immigration—or, more precisely, it doesn't do it powerfully enough. For some, it frees them to worry less about what is in their wallet and more about who may be moving into their neighborhoods or competing with them for jobs …
>
> The uncomfortable truth is that America's lack of a European-style welfare state hurts a lot of white Americans. But a large number of white voters believe that social spending programs mostly benefit nonwhites. As such, they oppose them with far more fervor than any similar voting bloc in Europe.
>
> In this context, tacking to the Left on economics won't give Democrats a silver bullet to use against the racial resentment powering Trump's success. It could actually wind up giving Trump an even bigger gun. If Democrats really want to stop right-wing populists like Trump, they need a strategy that blunts the true drivers of their appeal—and that means focusing on more than economics.

I would correct the last sentence: it means that they must fix their problem with good economics or be doomed to continued

The decay of social democratic parties

% of votes of social democratic parties in 18 Western European countries

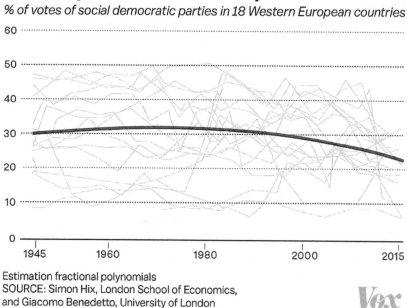

Estimation fractional polynomials
SOURCE: Simon Hix, London School of Economics,
and Giacomo Benedetto, University of London

marginalization. The Vox piece points out that since World War II, most European countries have adopted some model of social democracy: generous welfare states, regulated markets, high taxation, universal education, and socialized health care. The high-water mark of the political parties that embody that vision was in the 1970s.

They have all been losing support since that time. A Rightist revolt—not in a push against big-State policies but for a more nativist application of those same policies—began in France in the late 1970s and extended to Austria in the 1980s, and the movement has gained steam since the end of the Cold War through the new millennium. It is now rocking Europe from France to the Netherlands.

A study by Simon Hix and Giacomo Benedetto tracked the support for social democracy in 18 countries from 1945–2016. They find a long secular decline at the polls.

There is no reason to think this is going to reverse. The rise of the Right represents a repudiation of these policies, not in total, but in a particular form: the perception that the receivers represent a different tribe than the payers. Vox calls it "welfare chauvinism—an economic platform fairly similar to that of social democrats, but paired with an idea that immigrants should be excluded from receiving these benefits."

Vox sums it up: "If social democrats see their future as a competition for votes with right-wing populists, then they have two choices: lose the election, or lose their progressive identity."

The "Paradox of Social Democracy"

That's tough advice. On a deeper level, it means coming to terms with the greatest secret in lefty circles, still spoken about in hushed terms among mostly academic types. This secret might need to come out in the open now. It is this: two high values of the Left, diversity and welfare statism, are an unstable and electorally incompatible mix.

The problem is that the willingness to cough up taxes for a government bureaucracy to support people with whom you sense some identity draws on a tribal instinct. You might not love it but you put up with it because you somehow identify with the people on the receiving end. There but for the grace of God go you. But the less you personally identify with those on the receiving end, the less sympathetic you are and the less willing you are to pay.

This is a fascinating observation because the ethic of the welfare state pretends to be benevolent toward marginalized groups. In practice, it only works by bolstering and feeding on identity politics. The larger the welfare state, the more the payers demand that it only benefit others like themselves.

The more diverse the society, the less likely you are to feel as if your tribe is winning in this redistribution game. You are now vulnerable to political manipulation. The first demagogue to come along and say "look at the creeps who are winning at your expense" wins the game. It's an enormously powerful message. It taps into a deep sense of injustice that people have. Diversity becomes the proverbial straw that breaks the welfare camel's back.

What does this breakage look like? It looks exactly like what we see around the developed world: the rise of nativism, police state authoritarianism, the boiling up of racialist feelings and movements, protectionist trade policies, centralization of power in the hands of people who have no sympathy at all toward non-majority religions, races, and language groups.

In practice, this political dynamic can get really wicked. Social welfare states, such have been built since World War II, are only politically stable in exactly the kinds of societies that are incompatible with the kind of world the Left wants and the kind of people the Left believes we should be. That's a serious problem for them. It forces them to come to terms with a massive problem in their political worldview.

The Left Has No Answers

There seems to be no getting around this problem. Social democracy has created the very conditions that are leading to reactionary political movements that kick the left out of power. The left's own institutions easily get captured by movements that reject egalitarian values, and use those institutions to punish the people who built them.

And as I type those words, I'm reminded that F.A. Hayek actually warned of this exact problem in his 1944 book *Road to Serfdom*. He predicted that social democratic policies, despite being based on a humanitarian outlook, would actually end in feeding authoritarian political movements. He warned the world back then, but only now are thinkers on the left realizing that this is true and that they have a serious problem.

And keep in mind that this is not only about the demographic paradox. The roots go much deeper to a problem that traces back at least a century: namely that left-wing movements have a huge blind spot regarding economics. Their suspicion of free-market systems runs so deep that they can't come to terms with the obvious failure of the regulatory and welfare states they created. Or more precisely: despite all their failures, they cannot find their way toward a solution that would repudiate their foundational anti-capitalist impulses.

Just consider the obvious.

- They claim to love the poor and middle class. But when private enterprise comes along to bring food, clothing, and electronics to average people, via big-box stores, the left screams and denounces them. Instead of celebrating big box stores, fast food, and the mass availability of digital technology—which are actually achieving the old dream of universal access—they condemn them, regulate them, and even try to drive them out of existence.

- They claim to champion workers, but their taxes, mandates, wage floors, and restrictions have created a job marketplace that is hard to enter, restricted, leads to job locks, and pillages workers of their just compensation.

- They claim to champion the cause of democracy, but they create systems that prohibit average people from being the driving force for the society's use of resources.

- They want universal schooling and healthcare but create systems that are wildly costly, deliver inferior results, and deny average people the right to choose.

- They try to foment class war against the rich without acknowledging that many average people actually admire the rich and aspire to be like them, and need a system filled with opportunity to help them achieve those dreams.

In short, their egalitarian and democratic ideals are at odds with their refusal to appreciate economics and the role of the market in achieving their own professed ideals.

In saying that, I'm not just trying to score ideological points. There really is a tragedy here. Since at least the 1930s, if not decades earlier, left progressives decided to abandon their 19th-century ideals to embrace a statist means of organizing society. Their hatred of capitalism trumped their love of rights and freedoms, and now they are stuck with the results: their own institutions are being captured by interests hostile to their ideals.

Keeping Progress on Track

And at this point, there is no going back. They can't win. They are losing control. And there is no prospect that this is going to change unless there is some dramatic ideological shift. And this shift absolutely must take place, because the cause of liberty itself is in peril. It is being squeezed out of public life in a vice of right and left.

We need all hands on deck to keep human progress on track.

What form would this shift take? There are three paths, not necessarily mutually exclusive.

1. The social democrats need to lose their hostility to free enterprise, improve their economic understanding, and come out full force for deregulation, tax cuts, and privatization as the right means for realizing peace, prosperity, tolerance, and widespread access to material abundance.

2. The hard right needs to let go of its warm spot for the police state, migration restrictions, militarism, and middle-class welfare, and embrace a consistent view of human freedom that includes a tolerance for diversity and an acknowledgement that global trade is fully compatible with national pride.

3. We need a new and conscious movement that is devoted to a classical form of liberalism, applied in the 21st century. Such a movement should celebrate free enterprise, trade, and peace and recognize that the magic of freedom is revealed most profoundly in its capacity to create harmony out of diversity, strong cultural ties out of spontaneous association, and prosperity from the creative actions of individuals in an open-ended social order. Such a movement needs

to detach itself from the war between right and left and instead embrace liberty as the third way and the light in an otherwise dark world.

As implausible as it sounds, the third path seems most viable to me. In many ways, it really is 1946 again, a time that cries out for the emboldening of a passionate, dedicated, morally strong movement to save freedom from its enemies. A genuine liberal movement must not only reverse the multifarious errors of left and right from the past but also point the way toward a peaceful and flourishing future.

Open Your Eyes:
Social Democracy is Collapsing

A sign of strange times: *1984* by George Orwell has become a best-seller yet again. Here is a book distinguished for its dark view of the state, together with a genuine despair about what to do about it.

Strangely, this view is held today by the Right, the Left, and even people who don't think of themselves as loyal to either way. The whole fiasco happening in D.C. seems insoluble, and the inevitable is already taking place today as it did under the presidents who preceded Trump: the realization that the new guy in town is not going to solve the problem.

Now arrives the genuine crisis of social democracy. True, it's been building for decades but with the rise of extremist parties in Europe, and the first signs of entrenched and sometimes violent political confrontations in the United States, the reality is ever more part of our lives. The times cry out for some new chapter in public life, and a complete rethinking of the relationship between the individual and the state and between society and its governing institutions.

Origins of the Problem

At a speech for college students, I asked the question: who here knows the term social democracy? Two hands of more than one hundred went up. That's sad. The short answer is that social democracy is

what we have now and what everyone loves to hate. It's not constitu-
tionalism, not liberalism, not socialism in full, and not conservatism.
It's unlimited rule by self-proclaimed elites who think they know better
than the rest of us how to manage our lives.

By way of background, at the end of the Second World War, the
intellectual and political elites in the United States rallied around
the idea that ideology was dead. The classic statement summing up
this view in book form came in 1960: *The End of Ideology* by Daniel
Bell. A self-described "socialist in economics, a liberal in politics, and
a conservative in culture," he said that all wild-eyed visions of politics
had come to an end. They would all be replaced by a system of rule by
experts that everyone will love forever.

To be sure, the ultimate end-of-ideology system is freedom itself.
Genuine liberalism (which probably shouldn't be classified as an ideology at all) doesn't require universal agreement on some system of public administration. It tolerates vast differences of opinion on religion,
culture, behavioral norms, traditions, and personal ethics. It permits
every form of speech, writing, association, and movement. Commerce,
producing and trading toward living better lives, becomes the life-
blood. It only asks that people—including the state—not violate basic
human rights.

But that is not the end of ideology that Bell and his generation
tried to manufacture. What they wanted was what is today called the
managerial state. Objective and scientific experts would be given power
and authority to build and oversee large-scale state projects. These projects would touch on every area of life. They would build a cradle-to-
grave welfare state, a regulatory apparatus to make all products and
services perfect, labor law to create the perfect balance of capital and
labor, huge infrastructure programs to inspire the public (highways!
space! dams!), fine-tune macroeconomic life with Keynesian witch-
doctors in charge, a foreign-policy regime that knew no limits of its
power, and a central bank as the lender of last resort.

What Bell and that generation proposed wasn't really the end of ideology. It was a codification of an ideology called social democracy. It wasn't socialism, communism, or fascism as such. It was a gigantically invasive state, administered by elite bureaucrats, blessed by intellectuals, and given the cover of agreement by the universal right of the vote. Surely nothing can truly be oppressive if it is takes place within the framework of democracy.

A Brief Peace

The whole thing turned out to be a pipe dream. Only a few years after the book appeared, ideology came roaring back with a vengeance, mostly in reaction to the ossification of public life, the draft for the Vietnam war, and the gradual diminution of economic prospects of the middle class. The student movement rose up, and gained momentum in response to the violent attempts to suppress it. Technology gave rise to new forms of freedom that were inconsistent with the static and officious structure of public administration. Political consensus fell apart, and the presidency itself—supposed to be sacrosanct in the postwar period—was dealt a mighty blow with the resignation of President Richard Nixon. Government no longer held the high ground.

All that seemed to hold the old post-war social-democratic consensus together was the Cold War itself. Surely we should put aside our differences so long as our country faces an existential threat of Soviet communism. And that perception put off the unleashing of mass discontent until later. In a shocking and completely unexpected turn, the Cold War ended in 1989, and thus began a new attempt to impose a post-ideological age, if only to preserve what the elites had worked so hard to build.

This attempt also had its book-form definitive statement: *The End of History* by Francis Fukuyama. Fukuyama wrote, "What we may be witnessing is not just the end of the Cold War, or the passing of a particular period of post-war history, but the end of history as such: that is, the end point of mankind's ideological evolution and the universalization of Western liberal democracy as the final form of human government."

It was Bell 2.0 and it didn't last long either. Over the last 25 years, every institution of social democracy has been discredited, on both the Right and the Left, even as the middle class began to face a grim economic reality: progress in one generation was no longer a reliable part of the American dream. The last time a government program really seemed to work well was the moon landing. After that, government just became a symbol of the worst unbearable and unworkable burden. Heavily ideological protest movements began to spring up in all corners of American public life: the Tea Party, Occupy Wall Street, Black Lives Matter, Bernie, Trump, and whatever comes next.

The Core Problem

Every public intellectual today frets about the fracturing of American civic life. They wring their hands and wonder what has gone wrong. Actually, the answer is more simple than it might first appear. Every institution within this framework—which grew more bloated and imperious over time—turned out to be untenable in one or another sense. The experts didn't know what they were doing after all, and this realization is shared widely among the people who were supposed to be made so content by their creation.

Every program fell into one of three categories of failure.

1. **Financially unsustainable.** Many forms of welfare only worked because they leveraged the present against the future. The problem with that model is that the future eventually arrives. Think of Social Security. It worked so long as the few in older groups could pillage the numerous in younger groups. Eventually the demographics flipped so that the many were on the receiving end and the few were on the paying end. Now young people know that they will be paying their whole lives for what will amount to a terrible return

on investment. It was the same with Medicare, Medicaid, and other forms of fake "insurance" instituted by government. The welfare state generally took a bad turn, becoming a way of life rather than a temporary help. Subsidy programs like housing and student loans create unsustainable bubbles that burst and cause fear and panic.

2. **Terminally Inefficient.** All forms of government intervention presume a frozen world without change, and work to glue down institutions in a certain mode of operation. Public schools today operate as they did in the 1950s, despite the spectacular appearance of a new global information system that has otherwise transformed how we seek and acquire information. Antitrust regulations deal with industrial organization from years ago even as the market is moving forward; by the time the government announces its opinion, it hardly matters anymore. And you can make the same criticism of a huge number of programs: labor law, communications regulations, drug approvals and medical regulations, and so on. The costs grow and grow, while the service and results are ever worse.

3. **Morally unconscionable.** The bailouts after the 2008 financial crisis were indefensible to average people of all parties. How can you justify using all the powers of the federal government to feed billions and trillions overall to well-connected elites who were the very perpetrators of the crisis? Capitalism is supposed to be about profits and losses, not private profits and socialized losses. The sheer injustice of it boggles the mind, but this only scratches the surface. How can you pillage average Americans of 40% of their income while blowing the money on programs that are either terminally inefficient, financially unsustainable, or just plain wrong? How can a government expect to administer a comprehensive spying program that violates any expectation of privacy on the part of citizens? Then there is the problem of wars lasting decades and leaving only destruction and terror guerilla armies in their wake.

All of this can remain true without creating a revolutionary situation. What actually creates the tipping point in which social democracy morphs into something else? What displaces one failed paradigm with another? The answer lies with an even a deeper problem with social democracy. You can discern it from this comment by F.A. Hayek in 1939. "Government by agreement is only possible provided that we do not require the government to act in fields other than those in which we can obtain true agreement."

Agreement No More

Exactly. All public institutions that are politically stable—even if they are inefficient, offer low quality, or skirt the demands of basic morality—must at the minimum presume certain levels of homogeneity of opinion (at least) in the subject population; that is to say, they presume a certain minimum level of public agreement to elicit consent. You might be able to cobble this together in small countries with homogeneous populations, but it becomes far less viable in large countries with diverse populations.

Opinion diversity and big government create politically unstable institutions because majority populations begin to conflict with minority populations over the proper functions of government. Under this system, some group is always feeling used. Some group is always feeling put upon and exploited by the other. And this creates huge and growing tensions in the top two ideals of social democracy: government control and broadly available public services.

We created a vast machinery of public institutions that presumed the presence of agreement that the elites thought they could create in the 1950s but which has long since vanished. Now we live in a political environment divided between friends and foes, and these are increasingly defined along lines of class, race, religion, gender identity, and language. In other words, if the goal of social democracy was to bring about a state of public contentedness and confidence that the elites would take care of everything, the result has been the exact opposite. More people are discontented than ever.

F.A. Hayek warned us in 1944: when agreement breaks down in the face of unviable public services, strongmen come to the rescue. Indeed, I've previous argued that the smugness of today's social democrats is entirely unwarranted. Trump won for a reason: the old order is not likely coming back. Now the social democrats face a choice: jettison their multicultural ideals and keep their beloved unitary state, or keep their liberal ideals and jettison their attachment to rule by an administrative elite.

Something has to give. And it is. Dark and dangerous political movements are festering all over the Western world, built from strange ideological impulses and aspiring to new forms of command and control. Whatever comes of them, it will have little to do with the once-vaunted post-war consensus, and even less to do with liberty.

Presidential adviser Steve Bannon is a dark figure—straight out of Orwell—but he is smart enough to see what the Left does not see. He claims to want to use the Trump years to "deconstruct the administrative state." Notice that he doesn't say dismantle much less abolish; he wants to use it for different purposes, to build a new national collective under a more powerful executive.

The institutions built by the paternalistic, urbane, and deeply smug social democrats are being captured by interests and values with which they profoundly disagree. They had better get used to it. This is just the beginning.

The partisans of the old order can fight a hopeless battle for restoration. Or they can join the classical liberals in rallying around the only real solution to the crisis of our time: freedom itself. These are the ideological battle lines of the future, not Left vs. Right but freedom vs. all forms of government control.

The GOP Implosion
and the Rebirth of
(Classical) Liberalism

I just returned from a historic event, the nominating convention of the Libertarian Party. (I spoke but was not a delegate and declared no support for any particular candidate.) It was a thrilling, raucous, contentious, fun, serious, and, ultimately, an ebullient event filled with high drama and intense argument.

I had keynoted the last convention in 2014, and the difference between that event and this one was palpable. What made this one historic where the other was not? The remarkable events of this year within the two major parties have created an unprecedented opportunity. The sense of this was easily discernable. This was not a civic club. This was not a social gathering. This was not a liberty-themed meetup.

This is a political party. And it matters. The Trump takeover of the GOP, and the entrenched power of the Clinton machine with the Democrats, mean that people who are looking for freedom from power have nowhere within the system to go. This opens the possibility that a new and clear voice can be heard within national politics that points the way not toward more government control but toward the cause of human liberty itself.

What struck me, however, is how the big-picture significance of all of this was largely lost on most commentators and delegates at the

LP convention. Despite the ominous sense of responsibilities, they argued *ad infinitum* about ideology, theory, personality, and strategy. But I found few people who understood the full meaning of what is taking place.

What we have developing here is a new epoch in American politics: an authentically liberal (in the classical sense) political movement in the US is being born as an alternative to a deeply corrupt and ideologically dangerous mainstream dominated by two parties that have trended inexorably socialist and fascist.

In terms of mainstream politics, it's the interwar period all over again: brown shirts versus reds. Except for this: there is a way out this time. This new movement has a message that is clean and clear: enough is enough, let us be free. Freedom works; government power does not. The emergence of a national political party that stands for liberty might be necessary but it is surely not sufficient. It is a sign of the rise of a broader and potentially transformative social, cultural, and intellectual movement that offers a third way beyond left and right.

Labor, Tory, and Liberal

Consider the way politics has fleshed itself out in most developed democracies over the last 150 years. There have been three broad camps (or parties), which we can call Labor, Tory, and Liberal. The names of the first two have changed (left, right, socialist, fascist, Democrat, Republican, conservative, fake "liberal") but the themes have remained the same. The third force is known in most parts of the world as liberal except in the US where it is called libertarian today.

Labor was born in opposition to free markets, from the conviction that wealth was being wrongly distributed toward "capital" and at the expense of labor. This party has included labor unions, welfare statists, social democrats, socialists and even communists. It favors higher taxes, more regulatory control, and restrictions on commerce. Over time it came to represent the public sector bureaucracies and, finally, to embody every resentment against free enterprise you can dream up.

The Tories represent a different branch of the ruling class: the large banks, corporations, landed aristocracy, the dominant racial heritage, and the rich generally. They later came to include the interest groups that had a strong interest in an imperial foreign policy. This party had a different set of complaints against commercial freedom. It is too disruptive of tradition. It rewards the wrong people. It threatens business monopolies. The Tories long favored their own flavor of government control to restrain the "excesses" of freedom.

What the Tories and Labor have shared was a common desire to curb laissez faire based on conviction that society needs some plan emanating from the top, imposed by wise and public spirited people with the power to rule. In US history, these parties have had different names, but everyone knows them today as Democrats and Republicans. They have traded places many times but always moved toward the same general goal: an ever bigger state and ever less liberty.

The Liberal Party

And who are the Liberals? The liberal idea was born in the high middle ages and Renaissance, with the rise of commercial freedom and the prosperity that followed. It began with the realization that religious freedom is possible and need not send society reeling into chaos. The idea of freedom extended out during the Enlightenment to include speech, press, property rights, and foreign trade. By the 18th century, it came to include a love of peace and an aspiration for universal human rights.

Liberalism came of age in the 19th century, and its achievements were legion: social mobility for the whole population, new technologies of liberation, the end of slavery, the advance of women's rights, the vast expansion of income and living standards, the explosion of population. Its economic form was capitalism, the greatest generator of wealth for the masses of people ever discovered. The message of Liberalism was clear and exhilarating: all humans have rights that cannot be violated by the state, and, so long as this is the case, society can manage itself without authoritarian control.

It was a beautiful period, filled with optimism. But Liberalism had its enemies on the left and on the right. The storm clouds gathered and disaster struck in the 20th century. Liberalism was dealt a terrible blow by World War I and the government controls that followed in its wake. In the course of one decade in most parts of the developed world, we saw vast and sweeping victories against liberty as wrought by both the Labor and Tory forces: labor controls, income taxes, central banking, product regulation, racial segregation, zoning, marriage controls, speech controls, prohibitions, and imperialism as a national habit.

Even before the Great Depression kicked off unprecedented experiments in central planning and economic control, Liberalism had nearly vanished from politics, academia, and popular culture.

Ludwig von Mises was writing in Vienna at the time and attempted one last explanation of the Liberal philosophy. His brilliant 1927 book on the topic remains a statement for the ages. He pointed out that at this stage of history, all existing political parties represented a lobbying force for some segment of the population. Only liberalism, which had no party, represents the common interest of everyone. But given the size and scope of government, even he doubted that liberalism would return in his lifetime, and sadly he was right.

The Liberal Diaspora

Given this situation, where did the liberals to go? They were homeless by the time World War II broke out. Following the war, they had been largely driven out of national politics. They were excluded from legislative priorities and media culture, not to mention academia. So the handful that existed turned to writing, publishing, independent educational ventures, civic organizations, and think tanks.

A beautiful example of this was the establishment of the Foundation for Economic Education in 1946 by Leonard E. Read. He saw a need for liberalism to have a voice and made FEE its home. He preferred the term liberalism but, sadly, the term had been taken over by Labor and the left.

Read was the first in the post-war period to suggest the substitute term "libertarian" and, later, came to reject all labels in favor of what he called the "freedom philosophy."

By the early 1970s, the movement had grown to the point that it attempted its own political party. It was obvious that with Richard Nixon in control of the Republican Party, liberalism had no voice. The preferred name of Liberal was still taken, so a new party was named the Libertarian Party. Despite some small victories, it has never really taken hold as a viable competitor to the two major parties. (You can read a good timeline of the party here.)

The Union of Tory and Liberal

Still, the Liberal movement grew, under the influence of FEE and the Mont Pelerin Society, among many new upstarts. The names of their intellectual leaders are now household names among libertarians: Mises, Hayek, Rothbard, Rand, Lane, among many others.

In the 1980s, in the United States and the UK, the Tories were led by two individuals who adopted liberal rhetoric: Ronald Reagan and Margaret Thatcher. In both their platforms, we saw a fusion of concerns for individual freedom (focused on economic freedom) together with traditional Tory concerns for national security and restrictions on civil liberties.

This alliance of interests produced some remarkable results such as deregulation, tax reductions, reduced use of money printing, and freer trade. The results were brilliant by comparison to the malaise of the previous decade. Economic growth boomed. Technological innovations grew at an unprecedented pace. Such were the achievements not

of the Tory element of the administrations but of its liberal sectors, that
which curbed the growth of government and backed private enterprise,
thereby unleashing human creativity all over the developed world, and
inspiring a global revival of Liberalism.

Within living memory, the party of Liberalism came to be stuck
with this partnership. It has generally been beneficial, though muddy.
The message of freedom became mixed up with other concerns central
to Tory ideology: war, corporate monopoly, financial manipulation,
prohibitionism, and social control. To this day, this is a serious problem
for the Liberal party. We get stuck with the bad reputation of Tory policies, though we technically bear no responsibility for them.

The 21st Century Tory-Liberal Divorce

It was a long time coming but tensions finally boiled over in 2015
and finally with the apparent nomination of Trump in the spring
2016. Trump, representing an old Tory ideology devoid of the virtues
of Liberalism, reasserted the raw statism of interwar politics. His central pillars are familiar to anyone of a certain generation: mercantilism,
migration restriction, military belligerence, censorship, prohibition,
even to the point of praising internments and recalling a pre-Enlight-
enment view of religion and society.

It was as decisive as it was ugly: the liberal spirit had finally been
purged from the Republican party. There was no more room at the
table (and anyone who claims otherwise is not looking at reality). It
represents a repudiation of Reaganism, Thatcherism, and the coalition that drove the world to recovery. You only need to compare the
speeches of the Reaganites on economics and immigration with those
of Trump. They are worlds apart.

The shattering of this coalition is the single most significant political event of our times. It is done. It is a fact. It is decisive. And it will
change everything for the foreseeable future.

Liberalism Defines Itself

Just when everything seems lost, you look around and see something beautiful. For 45 years, activists have been struggling to keep the awkwardly named party alive. And it does live! It is on the ballot in every state. It has a full and well-developed platform. It is ready for action.

In the last six months, some awesome people stepped up, ready for the nomination at the top of the ticket. The results were not to every taste but still extraordinary in broad terms. The party rejected the extremes at all ends and voted to nominate two former governors as standard bearers, two men who speak plainly and clearly about freedom in all its forms.

People can complain about this particular issue or that one. But no one can dispute that both Gary Johnson and William Weld represent the Liberal spirit that is now called libertarian. The difference with the Republicans and Democrats is unmistakable. The LP is neither left not right, neither Labor nor Tory, but a third choice: Liberalism as traditionally understood. That is the ethos of the party and the message of its candidates to the American people and the world at large. It is a breath of fresh air.

In other words, believers in liberty are exactly where we need to be. It's a big tent, as it should be. It includes as many varieties of Liberalism as there are people who want to be free

And please remember: it's not just about politics. In fact, politics is the least of it. The LP (and I wish it were called the Liberal Party) is finally positioned to be the political voice of a cultural, social, and entrepreneurial resistance movement to the left (Labor, Democrat) and right (Tory, Republican). The takeover of the GOP by illiberal nativists/protectionists/authoritarians is what finally pushed it over the edge.

No, history does not end with this election. One could say that it is just now beginning, now that we finally have a choice, for the first time in our lives.

People often say that America has a two-party system. People always believe that the status quo will last forever. The truth is that the status quo always lasts until, suddenly, it doesn't.

Times are changing. Liberalism is back.

Take Back the Word "Liberal"

I would like to pick up an old campaign to take back the word "liberal" for the cause of human liberty. Or perhaps that's too ambitious. Perhaps it is enough for each of us to do our part not to keep conceding the use of this glorious word to the enemies of liberty. It does not belong to them. It belongs to us.

This is not a tedious argument over definitions; this is about the proper identification of a magnificent intellectual tradition. Liberalism is about human liberty and its gradual progress over the last 500 years. It is not about state control. In the coming year, I'm determined to at least make my own language reflect this reality.

Yes, I know this is an old campaign. It was a cause pushed by F.A. Hayek, Leonard Read, Frank Chodorov, John T. Flynn, Milton Friedman, and countless others.

My favorite case is Ludwig von Mises. In 1927, he wrote a book called *Liberalismus*. It was an attempt to recast and update the intellectual foundations of the entire liberal movement. To his knowledge, this had not yet been done.

"The greatness of the period between the Napoleonic Wars and the first World War," he wrote, "consisted precisely in the fact that the social ideal after the realization of which the most eminent men were striving was free trade in a peaceful world of free nations. It was an age of unprecedented improvement in the standard of living for a rapidly increasing population. It was the age of liberalism."

But by the time the English edition of his book came out in 1962, he worried that the word *liberal* had been lost. The book appeared under the title *The Free and Prosperous Commonwealth*. Very soon after, he changed his mind again. He had decided not to give up the great word, not because he was spiteful or belligerent or did not understand that language evolves. He decided that the term could not be given up.

"This usage is imperative," he wrote in 1966, "because there is simply no other term available to signify the great political and intellectual movement that substituted free enterprise and the market economy for the precapitalistic methods of production; constitutional representative government for the absolutism of kings or oligarchies; and freedom of all individuals from slavery, serfdom, and other forms of bondage."

Doesn't that just sum it up beautifully? The core conviction of liberalism was that society contained within itself the capacity for self-management. The social order was self-organized. We didn't need masters and slaves. Society did not need to be hierarchically organized. Everyone could have equal freedom. This was a radical idea, and it did indeed build the best of modernity as we know it.

Liberalism secured private property. It ended slavery. It brought equal freedom to women. It stopped wars of conquest. It broke down the class and caste systems. It freed speech. It stopped religious persecution. It opened economic opportunities for everyone. It cast moral disapproval on despotisms of all sorts.

It put the consumer in charge of production. It brought education, culture, leisure, and even luxury to the mass of men and women. It lengthened lives, brought down infant mortality, raised incomes, ended plagues and starvation, and ignited the fire of invention that gave humanity the ability to travel, communicate, and cooperate as never before and as one human family. It brought peace.

This is what liberalism did! How can we give up this word? We cannot. We will not.

It is because of liberalism's great achievements that the term itself became such a prize. We began to lose the word about 100 years ago, when the partisans of state power began to use the excuse of "liberalization" to push their agenda.

Gradually "liberalism" became about using public policy to create opportunities and improve the world, with the best of intentions. The statists' goals were the same as those of liberalism but the means they used to achieve their goals were completely antithetical and even dangerous to liberal ideals.

Matters became especially intense after the economic crash of 1929. Suddenly the market economy itself was on the hot seat and self-described liberals were forced to choose. Mostly they chose wrongly, and mainstream liberalism hooked up with big government and corporate statism. By the end of the New Deal, it was all over. The word had been stolen and came to mean the opposite of the original idea.

In the post-war period, there was a new coinage to describe people who opposed the political agenda of these new fake liberals. That word was "conservative," which was a highly unfortunate term that literally means nothing other than *to preserve*, an impulse that breeds reactionary impulses. Within this new thing called conservatism, genuine liberals were supposed to find a home alongside warmongers, prohibitionists, religious authoritarians, and cultural fascists.

It was a bad mix.

All these years later, this new form of liberalism remains intact. It combines cultural snobbery with love of statist means and a devotion to imposing the civic religion at all costs and by any means. And yes, it can be annoying as hell. This is how it came to be that the word *liberalism* is so often said with a sneer, which you know if you have ever turned on Fox News or Rush Limbaugh or Glenn Beck. And quite often, the right-wing attacks on liberalism are well deserved. But what does the right offer as an alternative? Not liberation but a new type of party control.

Given all these confusions, why not make another attempt to take back the word *liberalism*? Again, this is not an argument over the definition of a word. It is an argument about the proper means to build a great society. Is the goal of political life to maximize the degree of freedom that lives in the world, or is it to further tighten the realm of control and centrally plan our economic and cultural lives? This is the critical question.

The other advantage to using the word *liberalism* properly is that it provides an opportunity to bring up names like Thomas Jefferson, Adam Smith, Frédéric Bastiat, Lysander Spooner, Benjamin Tucker, Albert Jay Nock, Rose Wilder Lane, plus the more modern tradition with Rand, Mises, Rothbard, and Hayek, plus the tens of thousands of people who long for liberty today in academia, business, punditry, and public life generally. Just using the old term in its proper way provides an opportunity for enlightenment.

It's true that liberalism of the old school had its problems. I have my own issues with the positions of the old liberals, and they include a general naïveté over democracy, too great a tolerance for the mythical "night-watchman state," and some latent affection for colonialism.

The more important point is that genuine liberalism has continued to learn and grow and now finds a more consistent embodiment in what is often but awkwardly called *libertarianism* or *market anarchism*, both of which are rightly considered an extension of the old liberal intellectual project.

Still, even libertarians and anarcho-capitalists need to reattach themselves to the old word, otherwise their self-identifications become deracinated neologisms with no historical or broader meaning. Any intellectual project that is detached from history is finally doomed to become an idiosyncratic sect.

Let's just say what is true. Real liberalism lives. More than ever. It only needs to be named. It's something we can all do.

Bibliographic
and Biographic Note

The fast and furious rise of the alt-right in Europe, the UK, and the US has caught many people intellectually off-guard. I can speak for myself in this respect. My education and reading prepared me well to understand the statism of the left. My instincts became finely tuned. The threat to liberty from the right was always an abstraction: something that happened in history but had no present relevance.

Herein lies the danger of ever having considered yourself a completed intellectual. There is always more to know.

At some point in the last few years, something changed. It became impossible to ignore the rise of the collectivist right wing, one that rejects liberty and individualism in favor of statism and tribalism, that also claims to be the only viable alternative to the left. The war is on, and you see it everywhere: on campus, on social media, and even on the streets.

In retrospect, it's clear that the roots of this new movement are much deeper than, for example, the Trump campaign. There are sightings of the movement as far back as the early 1990s, and it is going to take some serious historical examination to trace all the forces and influences that led to it.

That's for later. For now, the most important step is to gain an understanding of this strange ideology and what it means for the free society. We need more than images of screaming marchers waving

Nazi flags. We need to understand the ideas behind it all (and this is true also for those who find themselves tempted by alt-right ideology). These ideas need to become real in our minds and thereby recognizable even when its adherents aren't giving Nazi salutes. We need a crash course in what I think is most accurately called right-Hegelianism. We need a conception of its roots, history, and meaning.

Mises the Anti-Fascist

The most important single work on right-collectivism is *Omnipotent Government* (1944) by Ludwig von Mises. The author himself, a lifetime opponent of socialism, was forced to flee his home in Vienna when the Nazi threat arrived. He left for Geneva in 1934 and came to the United States in 1940, where he went to work almost immediately, reconstructing the intellectual history and meaning of what was called fascism and Nazism.

The book appeared just as the war was ending. Here Mises reveals the economics, politics, and cultural appeal, as well as the conditions, that led to the Nazi rise. He deals very frankly with issues like trade, race, market integration, Jewry, discrimination, class resentment, imperialism, demographic control, trade, and the core illiberalism of rightist collectivism.

What you get out of this book: Mises will train your intellectual instincts to make sense out of what might seem like chaos around you. You will see patterns. You will see connections. You will see trajectories of thought and where they end up. In a strange way, then, the result of the book is to create a calming effect. It makes sense of the whole complicated mess. The book is also infused with an amazing and powerful passion that could only come from someone with his brilliance and direct and personal experience with the problem at hand.

F.A. Hayek the Anti-Fascist

My next choice is the most famous book that nobody today has read. It came out the same year as Mises's book. It is *The Road to Serfdom* by F.A. Hayek.

The usual interpretation of this book's core message—that the welfare state brings about socialism—is completely wrong. What Hayek actually argues is that socialism takes many forms, styles, and shades (red and brown, or left and right) and every variation results in the loss of freedom. You can believe you are fighting fascism with socialism and end up with a fascistic state, or you can fight socialism with fascism and end up with an authoritarian socialist state. He demonstrates that these really are false alternatives, and the only real and sustainable alternative to dictatorship is the free society.

Here again, Hayek had a profound personal interest in the outcome of the great ideological struggles of his time and understood them very well. He too was driven out of his home by the Nazi threat and landed in London where the academic scene was dominated by Fabian-style socialists who imagined themselves to be great fighters of fascism. Hayek shocked them all by calling them out: the system you want to manage society will actually bring about the very thing you claim to oppose. In other words, the book is not as much about the reds as it is about the browns and the threat that this way of thinking poses even to England and America.

In the course of his argument, he offers a basic tutorial in the functioning of freedom itself, which can never mean "rule by intellectuals" or "rule by intelligent social managers" but rather defers to the knowledge discovery process that characterizes the choices of individuals in society.

John T. Flynn the Anti-Fascist

The year 1944 also saw the publication of one of the greatest but least remembered attacks on fascism ever written: John T. Flynn's *As We Go Marching*.

Flynn was an amazing writer and thinker who came out of the anti-New Deal movement of the 1930s. This is his best and most scholarly work, with a full biography of Mussolini and a rich examination of fascist ideology. He provides the best list of traits of fascist politics I've seen. The message, in the end, is about how every warring state adopts fascist forms, with a specific accusation directed against Washington, D.C. In some ways, his message is similar to Hayek's but more tactile and focused.

Three years after the above books appeared, FEE founder Leonard Read came to Mises and asked him to write up a large essay that provides a one-stop shop for all things political that Mises had learned during his life. The manuscript grew and grew until it became a book that appeared in 1947: *Planned Chaos*. It's a masterpiece, one that bears reading and re-reading throughout your life.

I've looked far and wide for another essay from the period that directly connects Nazi experiments with American eugenics and failed to find one. Mises saw that relationship and called it out in several amazing passages. Directly relevant here are the sections on fascism and Nazism in particular. In brief form, he explains the roots of the terror in intellectual error.

The Terrible History

And this takes us directly to the hidden history of demographic planning in America. No understanding of right-Hegelianism and its implications can take shape without grappling with this weirdly hidden history.

Why is it so hidden and why has it taken 100 years to finally deal with the scandal that nearly the entire American ruling intellectual class was consumed by eugenic ideology for many decades before World War II? I suspect the reason is embarrassment about what happened. In particular, Progressives do not want to talk about this.

Eugenics is an inevitable outcome of any form of identitarianism that focuses on race and geography, as the alt-right does (the alt-left is the same!). If you can't control the "anarchy of human reproduction," all bets are off. In some ways, controlling birth is the first order of business for any form of rightist totalitarianism. That means: racism as an ideology and a statist tactic for managing the social order.

I'm always intrigued about the young boys on the streets shouting racist slogans and wearing MAGA hats, imagining that they are so politically incorrect. They have no idea that they are actually adopting the views of the entire American ruling class from a century ago that built the state they claim to hate. Indeed, most Americans know absolutely nothing about this history and how it was absolutely central to the building of the invasive and ubiquitous state that emerged out of the Progressive Era.

Progressivism Is Racism

The most important tutorial is Thomas Leonard's explosively brilliant *Illiberal Reformers: Race, Eugenics, and American Economics in the Progressive Era* (2016). This book (packed with footnotes that will keep you busy for weeks) documents how eugenic ideology corrupted the entire social science profession in the first two decades of the 20th century. Across the board, in the books and articles of the profession, you find all the concerns about race suicide, the poisoning of the national bloodstream by inferiors, and the desperate need for state planning to breed people the way ranchers breed animals. Talk about hidden history!

Now, you might say: these are Progressives, not rightists! It's true and that speaks to Hayek's point about red and brown being the inevitable expressions of factionalism with any single movement. The core point is that the word "progressive" here is ridiculously wrong. They were all reactionaries against the right of laissez-faire in the 19th century that drove such explosive demographic changes. It's one of the great ironies of intellectual/political history how the left and right blend into a single oppositional force to the free society.

This next book deals directly with this problem. It was a formative book for me personally because it answered a question I had long entertained but never answered. The question is this. Why was the free society overthrown so quickly and with such decisiveness and in such a short time, even though we were then surrounded by the evidence of the success of the free society? It's long been a mystery to me.

Snobbery and Statism

The answer is provided by John Carey's *The Intellectuals and the Masses: Pride and Prejudice Among the Literary Intelligentsia, 1880–1939* (2005) reveals a side to upper-class intellectuals in the UK that you didn't know existed. They despised the free market, not because it didn't work but because it did work. It was displacing the old aristocracy, transforming the cities, bringing the masses new consumer products, and transforming class relations. And they hated it. In other words, the revolt against laissez faire was fed by snobbery, and that led to the most extreme solution justified in the name of eugenics: the extermination of inferiors.

To see how this played out in the US, have a look at the harrowing and horrible evidence marshaled in Edwin Black's *War Against the Weak: Eugenics and America's Campaign to Create a Master Race* (2003, 2012). It shows how eugenics was central to Progressive Era politics. Laws requiring sterilization claimed 60,000 victims, but that was just the beginning. The entire nature and purpose of the regime changed in the direction of comprehensive social planning, a movement that is simply impossible to comprehend without realizing that eugenic and racist (and, inevitably, misogynistic) concerns were the driving force.

Jonah Goldberg's *Liberal Fascism* (2009) covers much of the same territory. It is an outstanding book that will continue to pay high returns for decades. The book is flawed, however, by the author's incessant to desire to blame everything that went wrong on the "left" and the "liberals" (talk about a misnomer!). His refusal to acknowledge the broadness of the eugenic movement and its diverse ideological expressions—which were fundamentally conservative in motivation—makes the whole book come across like some partisan attack. If only he had admitted that the revolt against laissez faire took on many colorings, the book would have made a much more powerful statement for freedom and against statism in all its forms.

Right-Hegelianism also takes religious forms. It begins with a small sect that believes its religion has been unbearably corrupted by modernity and seeks out ancient texts as guides to reconstructing it in a purer if forgotten form. The results depart from the organic development of the faith in question to embrace a rationalist reconstruction.

It has great leaders that builds a movement focused on some great restorative act that involves coercion and the invention of a rationale for every manner of immortality. Such movements have popped up in the 20th century within varieties of religious expression, including Catholicism, Protestantism, Judaism, Islam, Magic, and Occultism. The strange guide here is Mark Sedgwick's *Against the Modern World: Traditionalism and the Secret Intellectual History of the Twentieth Century*.

That's the main list, the books that open up a new world of intellectual exploration and shine so much light on where we are today. More valuable, still, is reading the original works of these thinkers, from Johann Fichte to Friedrich List to John Ruskin to Madison Grant to Carl Schmitt and beyond. The loathing of liberalism is never more obvious than when experienced firsthand. This is best way to get into their heads and understand (and thereby combat) their worldview.

Champions of freedom need to have a broad view of the threats we face and that requires some serious study. Then the next step is just as important: develop a new vision of the kind of person you want to become so you can make the largest possible contribution to the society we want to see around us.

A major project of mine for the last three years has been to trace the origin and development of the ideas that led to today's alt-right activists. They have emerged on the political scene suddenly and with impressive ferocity. Some people just assume that they represent nothing but a melange of hate and racism.

This is too simple. Even the most dumbed-down political movement is built by slaves of defunct philosophers. But which ones? And does the worldview cohere to the point that we can anticipate the patterns and policies of this group?

To reconstruct the history of this school of thought is not easy. It is not usually thought of as a school of thought in the way we think of Marxism, for example. A half-century has passed since these ideas have been a pressing issue.

What's In a Name?

What do we call this school of thought? Following Ludwig von Mises, I prefer the designation right-Hegelian, but there are plenty of other terms that could apply, including fascist, national socialist, right-collectivist, and so on.

What we are looking for here is a distinct (and ultimately predictable) collection of attitudes concerning the individual and the state. It is historicist, believing that the narrative of time is driving us toward some end state. It is nationalist. It is identitarian: usually about race but also about religion, gender identity, and intelligence. It believes that commerce should track identity and nation, not economic interest. It is also statist: its vision of what society should do and look like requires mass violence to achieve.

It has nothing to do with the traditional liberalism of Adam Smith or John Locke, or the conservatism of Edmund Burke, Joseph De Maistre, or Machiavelli. It departs dramatically from those models to long for a full reconstruction of the state and society, to make it conform to an edgy drama of how life should be. In this way, it is a twin of Marxism, just with a different cultural feel and moving ideological pieces.

Another way to think of this list: if you are tempted by the alt-right, here is your family tree. Do you like what you see?

Slaves of Philosophers

To come up with this list, I've followed breadcrumbs left by Mises and Hayek and modern authors Tom Palmer and Thomas Leonard. Here is my best effort at a short biographical list, based on each person's pivotal influence:

Johann Fichte (May 19, 1762 – January 27, 1814) studied theology at the University of Jena, wrote theological laudatory works such as *Foundations of Natural Right*, and was a professor and rector at Humboldt University, and became a dedicated opponent of liberalism, later most revealed in his fascist "Addresses to the German Nation."

G.F. Hegel (August 27, 1770 – November 14, 1831) received his theological certificate from Tübingen Seminary and taught philosophy at Jena, Heidelberg, and the University of Berlin. His followers split into left- and right-wing branches that adopted his theory of history, which culminated in one or another form of anti-liberal statism.

Friedrich List (August 6, 1789 – November 30, 1846) worked as an administrative professor at the University of Tübingen but was expelled and went to America where he became involved in the establishment of railroads and championed an economic "National System" or industrial mercantilism.

Thomas Carlyle (December 4, 1795 – February 5, 1881) was a Scottish philosopher who wrote books such as *On Heroes, Hero-Worship, and The Heroic in History*, *The French Revolution: A History*, defended slavery and dictatorship, and coined the term "the dismal science" for economics precisely because economics opposed slavery.

John Ruskin (February 8, 1819 – January 20, 1900) was the leading English art critic of the Victorian era, a philanthropist, became the first Slade Professor of Fine Art at Oxford University, and founded the Guild of Saint George in opposition to commercial capitalism and mass production for the masses.

Houston Stewart Chamberlain (September 9, 1855 – January 9, 1927) traveled around Europe and, becoming highly enamored of Wagner and German culture, and a leading Hitler celebrant. He advocated blood-thirsty anti-Semitism and wrote *The Foundations of the Nineteenth Century* which emphasized Europe's Teutonic roots.

Frederick Hoffman (May 2, 1865 – 1946) was born in Germany, became a statistician in America, and wrote *The Race Traits and Tendencies of the American Negro* characterizing African-Americans as inferior to other races, but casting aspersions on Jews and non-caucasians. The monograph was published by the American Economic Association.

Madison Grant (November 19, 1865 – May 30, 1937) graduated from Yale University and received a law degree from Columbia Law School, after which his interest in eugenics led him to study the "racial history" of Europe and write the popular hit book *The Passing of the Great Race*. He was a leading environmentalist and a champion of nationalized forests, for strange eugenic reasons.

Charles Davenport (June 1, 1866 – February 18, 1944) was a professor of zoology at Harvard who researched eugenics, wrote *Heredity in Relation to Eugenics*, and founded the Eugenics Record

Office and International Federation of Eugenics Organizations. He was a major player in the construction of the eugenic state.

Henry H. Goddard (August 14, 1866 – June 18, 1957) was a psychologist, a eugenicist, the Director of Research at the Vineland Training School for Feeble-Minded Girls and Boys. He popularized IQ studies and turned them into a weapon used by the state to create a planned society, creating hierarchies determined and enforced by public bureaucrats.

Edward A. Ross (December 12, 1866 – July 22, 1951) received a Ph.D. from University of John Hopkins, was part of the faculty at Stanford, and became a founder of sociology in the United States. Author of *Sin and Society* (1905). He warned of the dysgenic effects of permitting women freedom of choice to engage in commercial work and pushed laws to prohibit women's work.

Robert DeCourcy Ward (November 29, 1867 – November 12, 1931) was a professor of meteorology and climatology at Harvard University and co-founded the Immigration Restriction League, fearing the dysgenic effects of Slavic, Jewish, and Italian intermarriage. His influence was key to the closing of borders in 1924, trapping millions in Europe to be slaughtered.

Giovanni Gentile (May 30, 1875 – April 15, 1944) was an Italian neo-Hegelian idealist philosopher, who provided an intellectual foundation for Italian Fascism and helped write *The Doctrine of Fascism* with Benito Mussolini. He was briefly beloved by the American press for his intellect and vision.

Lewis Terman (January 15, 1877 – December 21, 1956) was a eugenicist who focused on studying gifted children as measured by IQ. Ph.D. from Clark University, he became a member of the pro-eugenic Human Betterment Foundation, and was president of the American Psychology Association. He pushed strict segregation, coerced sterilization, immigration controls, birthing licenses, and a planned society generally.

Oswald Spengler (May 29, 1880 – May 8, 1936) graduated from Halle University, Germany became a teacher, and in 1918 wrote *Decline of the West* on historical cycles and changes that sought to explain Germany's defeat in the Great War. He urged a new Teutonic tribal authoritarianism to combat liberal individualism.

Ezra Pound (October 30, 1885 – November 1, 1972) was an expat modernist poet from America who converted to national socialism and blamed WWI on usury and international capitalism and supported Mussolini and Hitler during WWII. A brilliant but deeply troubled man, Pound used his genius to write for Nazi newspapers in England before and during the war.

Carl Schmitt (July 11, 1888 – April 7, 1985) was a Nazi jurist and political theorist who wrote extensively and bitterly against classical liberalism for the ruthless wielding of power (*The Concept of the Political*). His view of the state's role is total. He admired and celebrated despotism, war, and Hitler.

Charles Edward Coughlin (October 25, 1891 – October 27, 1979), was a massively influential Canadian-American priest who hosted a radio show with 30 million listeners in the 1930s. He despised capitalism, backed the New Deal, and plunged into hard anti-Semitism and Nazi doctrine, publishing speeches by Goebbels under his own name. His show inspired thousands to protest in the streets against Jewish refugees.

Julius Caesar Evola (May 19, 1898 – June 11, 1974) was a radically traditionalist Italian philosopher who focused on history and religion and worshipped violence. He was admired by Mussolini and wrote adoring letters to Hitler. He spent a lifetime advocating for the subjugation of women and holocaust for Jews.

Francis Parker Yockey (September 18, 1917 – June 16, 1960) was an American attorney and dedicated Nazi who wrote *Imperium: The Philosophy of History and Politics* which argues for a culture-based, totalitarian path for the preservation of Western culture against the influence of the Jews. He said the fall of the Third Reich was a temporary setback. He killed himself in prison where he was being held for passport fraud.

It was Yockey who had a powerful influence on **Willis Carto** (1926–2015), the primary agitator for fascist/Nazi theory and practice in post-war US media, founder of publishing outfits and institutions that kept Nazi doctrine alive for decades. He, along with a few other devoted Nazis, is the actual organizational bridge from pre-war to post-war Nazi theory and practice.

Those are the main players. What about today's alt-right? The names are well known by now but it is probably too soon to discern which among the bad boys of the alt-right wield decisive influence and which are just along for the ride. What matters much more is that even they are largely unaware of the deep heritage of their belief system, which for two hundred years has taken a hard stand against anything most people would recognize as freedom.

About FEE

The Foundation for Economic Education (FEE) is the premier source for understanding the humane values of a free society and the economic, legal, and ethical principles that make it possible. At FEE, you'll be connected with people worldwide who share those values and are inspired by the dynamic ideas of free association, free markets, and a diverse civil society.

Explore freedom's limitless possibilities through seminars, classroom resources, social media, free online courses, and exciting daily content at FEE.org. Learn how your creativity and initiative can result in a prosperous and flourishing life for yourself and the global community. Whether you are just beginning to explore entrepreneurship, economics, or creating value for others or are mentoring others on their journeys, FEE has everything you need.

FEE is supported by voluntary, tax-deductible contributions from individuals, foundations, and businesses who believe that it is vital to cultivate a deep appreciation in every generation for individual liberty, personal character, and a free economy.

WE INVITE YOU TO ADVANCE LIBERTY WITH US.

The Foundation for Economic Education is the premier source for understanding the humane values of a free society, and the economic, legal, and ethical principles that make it possible. At FEE, students and their mentors explore freedom's limitless possibilities through seminars, classroom resources, social media, daily content, and free online courses, all available at *FEE.org*.

FEE.ORG |

CPSIA information can be obtained
at www.ICGtesting.com
Printed in the USA
BVHW041810210620
582011BV00014B/463